# SIZE
# DOES
# MATTER

# THE MAKING OF
# GODZILLA™

## RACHEL ABERLY
### FOREWORD BY VOLKER ENGEL

**HarperPrism**
*A Division of HarperCollins Publishers*

OTHER GODZILLA™ BOOKS FROM ▦ HarperPrism

■ GODZILLA™ Based on the Screenplay by Dean Devlin & Roland Emmerich • Novelization by Stephen Molstad

■ THE GODZILLA™ MOVIE POSTCARD BOOK

■ THE MAKING OF GODZILLA™ Rachel Aberly

▦ HarperPrism
A *Division of* HarperCollins*Publishers*
10 East 53rd Street, New York, N.Y. 10022–5299

Set Photography: *Claudette Barius, Sam Urdank, Myles Aronowitz*

Effects Photography (Centropolis Effects/CFX): *Isabella Vosmikova, Volker Engel, Michael Sean Foley*

Building Miniature Photography: *Matthew Gratzner and Seth Curlin*

CG Image Photography (Viewpoint DataLabs): *Joe Putnam, Putnam Photography*

Preproduction Paintings: *Mauro Borelli, Sean Hargreaves, Patrick A. Janicke, Tom Lay*

Tatopoulos Model Shop Photography: *Claudette Barius*

Storyboard Rendering: *Peter Ramsey, Kevin McCarthy, John Mann, Eric Ramsey*

Book Design and Production: *Jeannette Jacobs*

Library of Congress Cataloging-in-Publication Data
Aberly, Rachel.
The making of Godzilla / Rachel Aberly.
p.   cm.
ISBN 0-06-107317-2
1. Godzilla (Motion picture : 1998)     I. Title.
PN1997.G56834A23   1998
791.13'72--DC21                                    98-3579
                                                            CIP
ISBN 0–06–107317–2

HarperCollins®, ▦®, and HarperPrism® are trademarks of HarperCollins*Publishers* Inc.

First paperback printing: June 1998
Printed and bound in Canada

For more information about GODZILLA, log onto the World Wide Web at
http://www.GODZILLA.com or at www.sony.com

Visit HarperPrism on the World Wide Web at http://www.harperprism.com

10 9 8 7 6 5 4 3 2 1

# ACKNOWLEDGMENTS

There are a lot of people who helped make this book possible. We'd like to take this opportunity to thank them for their efforts.

## CENTROPOLIS PRODUCTIONS

Dean Devlin, Producer and Writer
Roland Emmerich, Director, Writer, and Executive Producer
Volker Engel, Visual Effects Supervisor
Ute Emmerich, Executive Producer
Bill Fay, Executive Producer
Peter Winther, Co-producer
Kelly Van Horn, Co-producer
Dionne McNeff, Executive in Charge of Production
Rachel Olschan, Assistant to Dean Devlin and Dionne McNeff
Tavin Marin, Assistant to Dean Devlin
Will Plyler, Assistant to Bill Fay
Giles Gordon, Assistant to Volker Engel
Lisa Di Santo, Assistant to Rachel Aberly

## SONY PICTURES ENTERTAINMENT/ TRISTAR PICTURES

John Calley, President and Chief Operating Officer
Robert Levin, President, Worldwide Marketing
Christopher Lee, President of Production
Ray Zimmerman, Senior Vice-President, Production Administration
Eric Baum, Senior Counsel, TriStar Pictures

## SONY SIGNATURES LICENSING

Peter Dang, Executive Vice-President
Patrick Kelly, Vice President, Business Affairs and Legal Counsel

Anita Frazier, Vice-President, Domestic Licensing Sales
Laetitia May, Director, Product Development
Cindy Irwin, Manager, Product Development
and LaDonna Williams

## TOHO COMPANY, LTD.

Masaharu Ina, General Manager
Yukio Kotaki, Manager

## HARPERPRISM & HARPERCOLLINS

John Silbersack,
John Douglas, Noelle LaCorbiniere, Rich Miller
Dianne Walber, Janet Millar
Susan McDonough, Donna Cullen-Dolce, Tom Finnegan
C. Linda Dingler, Jeannette Jacobs, Nyamekye Waliyaya
Gene Mydlowski, Carl Galian, Annamaria Grilli

## CENTROPOLIS EFFECTS

Steven Puri, President
Steffen Wild, CG Supervisor
Carolin Quis, CG Supervisor
Karen Goulekas, Associate Visual Effects Supervisor
Andy Jones, Animation Supervisor
Fiona Bull, Digital Effects Producer

## PERFORMERS:

Matthew Broderick
Jean Reno
Hank Azaria
Maria Pitillo
Kevin Dunn
Doug Savant
Vicki Lewis
Arabella Field
Michael Lerner
Harry Shearer
Malcolm Danare

## ON THE PRODUCTION

Ueli Stieger, Cinematographer
Kim Winther, Second Unit Director
Joe Sanchez, Assistant Cameraman
Jim Grce, Gaffer
P. Gary Krakoff, Construction Coordinator
Terry Clotiaux, Visual Effects Producer
Bob Hurrie, Visual Effects Producer
Joseph Porro, Costume Designer
Oliver Scholl, Production Designer
Emmet Kane, Special Effects Foreman
Ken Fix, Supervising Location Manager
Terry Ciccarelli, Model Maker
Kim Berner, Script Supervisor
R. A. Rondell, Stunt Coordinator
David Siegel, Film Editor
Peter Amundson, Film Editor
Peter Elliott, VFX Editor
Joe Viskocil, Miniature Special Effects Supervisor, Head Pyrotechnician
Tricia Mulgrew, Data Wrangler
Joe Jackman, Data Wrangler

## TATOPOULOS DESIGN, INC.

Patrick Tatopoulos
Guy Himber, Mechanical Department Supervisor
Oana Bogdan, Creature Art Director

## HUNTER GRATZNER INDUSTRIES

Matthew Gratzner
Shannon Blake Gans

## VIEWPOINT DATALABS

Walter Noot, Scotti McGowan

## QUEBECOR PRINTING

Claudette Gauvin
Michael Mclaren
Guy Archambault

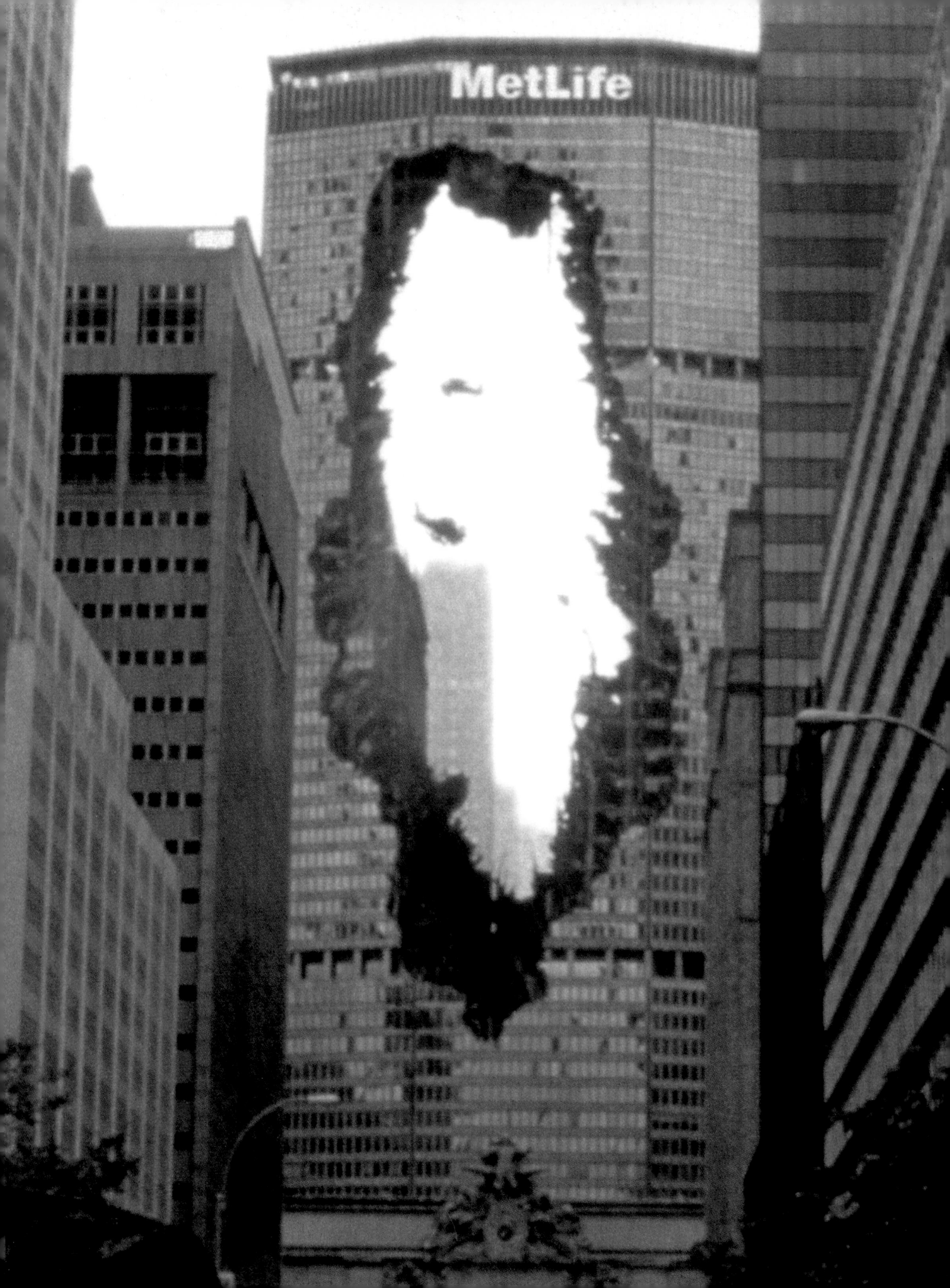
MetLife

# F OREWORD

## SPRING OF 1972

Leaving the lobby of the Apollo theater in my German hometown
Bremerhaven, my father and I stepped into the twilight of a rainy
afternoon.

I had just seen *Destroy All Monsters*, my first Godzilla movie. It
was a revelation: I wanted to be a part of the film industry. Life
would never be the same again. I was seven years old.

Several years later I had seen more than a dozen other movies
with Godzilla, all of them on the big screen. This gave me the
chance to study the special effects really close and I started to
distinguish between good and bad model shots and was sheepishly
happy whenever I spotted the wires from which a lot of the models
were hung.

I saved money to buy my first 8mm camera, to try out all these
different film tricks for myself: model photography, slow motion
effects and small pyrotechnical gags (mostly with firecrackers). I
did drawn animation, puppet animation, studied graphic design and
film. In 1989 director Roland Emmerich hired me as a modelmaker
on his German film *Moon 44*. Eventually I became the project's
effects supervisor.

## SPRING OF 1996

In midst the hectic days of supervising the digital postproduction
for *Independence Day*, the writer/producer/director-team Roland
Emmerich and Dean Devlin approached me with the question, if I
would consider to do another project with them: *Godzilla!*

All of a sudden I felt like being seven years old again, being
given the chance to create state-of-the-art effects for a new movie
with the world's most famous monster.

It was the beginning of a childhood dream becoming true.

One thing was clear from the beginning: It wouldn't be a cheesy,
campy *Godzilla*. The goal was clearly to create a creature that would
look on hundred percent believable to the trained eye of the
sophisticated movie audience of the nineties. The fact that Patrick
Tatopoulos' creature design was loved by all parties involved from
the beginning, showed that everything was leading in the right
direction. The *ID4* team was back together again and Centropolis
Effects, a company that would do most of the digital
postproduction, was founded.

As the visual effects supervisor on *Godzilla*, my task could be

best described as being the director for everything that could not be shot "live-action" with the actors on location or on a soundstage. From a pure job point of view it meant seventeen months of hard work with no days off and no private life.

Of course there was more to it. It was a journey through the amazing realms of modern filmmaking, described best with Rutger Hauer's words in the movie *Blade Runner*:

I have seen things, you people wouldn't believe. . .

And I saw this:

- hundreds of nine-foot-tall eggs inside a gigantic set on L.A.'s largest soundstage,

- Matthew Broderick standing in front of a huge fish pile in front of New York's Flatiron Building

- the dawn over Manhattan from a helicopter while circling the Empire State Building

- the destruction of the Brooklyn Bridge

- a swimming fish-factory, as large as a supertanker, being sunk in six seconds via hydraulics in a tank in the California desert

- the gigantic interiors of a subway ventilation shaft
- tanks in Central Park and staged chaos with hundreds of extras on 42$^{nd}$ Street
- the fiery destruction of the Madison Square Garden on a parking lot
- and of course an old childhood friend of mine: The "King of the Monsters" himself

When Japanese producer Tomoyuki Tanaka, director Inoshiro Honda, and effects wizard Eiji Tsuburaya filmed the original *Gojira* in 1954, they created *the*

classic monster movie. It is an honor for me to walk in Tsuburaya's footprints, having the chance to use traditional effects and high-end computer animation at the same time to get the best of both worlds.

This journey gave me the opportunity to work with some of the best modelmakers, computer-artists, camera-specialists, lighting crew, pyrotechnicians, designers, editors, and producers in this business. It also gave me the extraordinary experience to work with digital mavin Karen Goulekas, who, as Associate Visual Effects Supervisor was clearly the driving force on the pixelfront.

As a die-hard *Back to the Future* fan I have to admit that every Marty McFly needs his Doc Brown.

Thank you Roland and Dean for pulling me onto the magic carpet.

A couple of months after the movie has opened in the US, I will fly back to my hometown to see the film with my family. With a little luck it will be a rainy afternoon and when I see a little boy with his father coming out of the movie theater, I will think to myself: *I am the luckiest guy in the world.*

—*Volker Engel, Visual Effects Supervisor,*
*Marina Del Rey, February 1998*

# A DEVASTATING, BLINDING FLASH OF WHITE LIGHT FILLS THE SKY.

The Pacific Ocean churns, engulfing a freighter with wicked speed.

Giant footprints plow an ominous path through miles of Panamanian forests and beaches.

Ships off the U.S. coast capsize, dragged into an inexplicably roiling sea, where they are instantly and totally demolished.

This profound and utter destruction heads inexorably toward a small, densely populated island called Manhattan. Swiftly and silently it approaches, an enormous beast that comes to be known as Godzilla.

This towering creature relentlessly smashes through Manhattan, leaving a trail of ruin and panic in its terrible wake. The army mobilizes, aiming its most advanced weaponry at the monster, to no avail. This giant menace proves to be a wily and elusive target. Its defeat will require something beyond mere artillery: a scientist studying the effects of the atomic accident in Chernobyl, an ambitious TV reporter and a reckless cameraman, a veteran colonel and his earnest, inexperienced sergeant, an enigmatic French insurance investigator. The devastating monster draws them all into an odd and shifting alliance. Despite their often conflicting agendas and motives, they must join forces to unravel the mystery behind this incredible creature, to stop it before it is too late.

*Godzilla*, the undisputed king of movie monsters, has been updated for the screen by Roland Emmerich and Dean Devlin, the filmmakers behind the box office phenomenon, *Independence Day*. Emmerich directs and Devlin produces an original screenplay they co-wrote. The film stars Matthew

■ ABOVE: *Sounding alarm on a Japanese fish-factory ship.*

■ INSET LEFT: *A fisherman swims as his boat bobs to the surface.*

■ RIGHT TOP: *Flooding corridor on the fish-factory ship as Godzilla's claws let in the sea.*

■ BELOW: *Broderick looking out of giant footptint.*

Broderick as the earnest scientist Dr. Nick Tatopoulos and Jean Reno as the enigmatic Phillipe Roache. *Godzilla* also stars Hank Azaria as the intrepid cameraman Animal, who helps his friend Audrey, a determined, inexperienced reporter, played by Maria Pitillo. Also featured are Harry Shearer as Charles Caiman, a pompous television reporter; Michael Lerner as the beleaguered mayor of New York; Doug Savant as the gritty, occasionally overwhelmed Sergeant O'Neal and Kevin Dunn as his principled, stoic superior, Colonel Hicks; Vicki Lewis as the brilliant Dr. Elsie Chapman; and Arabella Field as Lucy, Audrey's best friend and Animal's patient, if vociferous, wife.

    *Godzilla* is executive produced by Roland Emmerich, Ute Emmerich, and William Fay. Peter Winther and Kelly Van Horn are co-producers. A Centropolis Entertainment/Woods Entertainment/Fried Entertainment production, the film will be released by TriStar Pictures. Cinematographer is Ueli Steiger. Production designer is Oliver Scholl. Joseph Porro is

■ LEFT: *The water swells.*

11

the costume designer. Visual effects supervisor is Volker Engel. Creature effects are by Tatopoulos Design, Inc. Centropolis Effects (along with several other houses) will create the digital effects. TriStar Pictures released the film on May 20, 1998.

Perhaps one of the world's most famous and beloved monsters, Godzilla, first appeared in Japan with the 1954 release *Gojira*. An American version of the film was released in the United States in 1956 as *Godzilla, King of the Monsters*, which starred Raymond Burr and Takashi Shimura.

Godzilla looms large, in several respects. He went on to star in twenty-two films. Only that urbane secret agent 007 has appeared in more films. Not merely prolific, Godzilla's appeal is universal; the creature boasts a ninety-five percent recognition rating across the globe. Godzilla has always proved to be an overwhelming adversary, whether battling such foes as the Smog Monster or merely through Tokyo. It was, in fact, Godzilla's monumental status (he stood one

hundred sixty-four feet high in the first film) that intrigued Emmerich and Devlin. After all, the filmmakers had to follow up *Independence Day*, which established new worldwide box office records. By the first day of principal photography on *Godzilla*, *Independence Day* had surpassed $800,000,000 in total global receipts.

"Because of the phenomenal reaction to *Independence Day*, Roland and I were fortunate enough to travel around the world to promote it. It seemed that in every country, we were asked the same question: How do you follow up a movie like *Independence Day*? It was a really tough question to answer. The only thing that seemed remotely in the ballpark was *Godzilla*. It afforded us the opportunity to do something bigger, wilder, and more amazing than we'd ever attempted before," Dean Devlin says.

TriStar Pictures, the studio which financed and released the picture, had negotiated with Godzilla's creators, Toho Co. Ltd., to obtain the rights to the legendary monster. TriStar President of Production Chris Lee, then the executive in charge of the project, harbored a childhood affection for the great beast.

"I grew up in Hawaii and I actually watched the *Godzilla* movies in a Toho theater. I saw the original Japanese version there, as well as the subsequent ones, and I always thought that I'd love to see another *Godzilla* movie, though when I started doing this in 1991–92, I don't remember getting much

■ ABOVE: *Animal (Hank Azaria).*
■ FAR LEFT TOP: *Phillipe Roache (Jean Reno).*
■ FAR LEFT BOTTOM: *Volker Engel in close-up.*
■ LEFT: *Emmerich sets up Madison Square Garden ticket booth scene.*
■ RIGHT TOP: *Audrey (Maria Pitillo).*
■ RIGHT BOTTOM: *Dr. Elsie Chapman (Vicki Lewis).*

GODZILLA LOOMS LARGE, IN SEVERAL RESPECTS.

HE WENT ONTO STAR IN TWENTY-TWO FILMS.

encouragement. It was a film that I had always wanted to do, but I wasn't exactly sure quite how to accomplish it. I knew that I wanted to tell a story that was done straight-ahead, in the spirit of the first movie, which was not campy. I wanted to reflect not what the movie had become but how it started out. I loved the goofier

*Godzillas*, too, but I knew a new version was about taking it seriously. You can't consciously set out to make it campy."

Lee contracted two screenwriters, Ted Elliot and Terry Ruscio, who, Lee says, "came up with a fantastic script." Their story also appealed to Director Jan De Bont.

"Jan De Bont signed on as director, following (the release of) *Speed*, which was a great coup. We worked together for about, oh, six months in pre-production as well as on the screenplay, but at the end of the day, the budget was more than we were willing to spend and Jan felt very strongly that this was the way to make the movie. So, we parted company and he went on to make *Twister*, along the way taking the cast originally meant for *Godzilla* to do that movie," Lee says. (Actress Helen Hunt was among this cast. In a nice turn of events, her boyfriend and fellow thespian Hank Azaria went on to star in Emmerich and Devlin's *Godzilla*.) At this point, Lee turned to Emmerich and Devlin, whom he had known for a long time, ever since Emmerich had pitched Lee one of his early movies, *Moon 44*. Emmerich had hired Devlin to act in that film and they forged their filmmaking partnership during that shoot. Lee later worked with Emmerich and Devlin when TriStar distributed the duo's first American film, *Universal Soldier,* and always wanted to collaborate with them again. *Godzilla* offered that opportunity.

"I think they do these kind of movies really well because they have their finger on the pulse of the public," Lee muses. "And they can synthesize elements of pop culture that we've all grown up on — the idea of an alien invasion, the notion of

■ LOWER RIGHT: *Roland Emmerich directing the mayor (Michael Lerner).*

■ UPPER NEAR RIGHT: *Sergeant O'Neal (Doug Savant).*

■ UPPER FAR RIGHT: *Bill Fay & Peter Winther.*

■ LEFT BOTTOM: *Co-producer/UPM Kelly Van Horn.*

■ LEFT TOP: *Dr. Mendel Craven (Malcome Danare).*

■ LEFT INSET: *Dean Devlin.*

Area 51. They can take an icon like Godzilla and keep the essence of what is best from what was popular and has become sort of cheesy over time and reinvent it. They stay true to the myth but reinvent it for current audiences. And they never forget the humor, not broad humor but comedy that comes out of situations. They're great storytellers and while they provide amazing visual set pieces, they recognize that those effects must always be in service of the story and characters. They never talk down to their audiences and they understand what they're doing, which is broad-based, event entertainment. So, I thought they'd be perfect for *Godzilla*."

"The challenge of *Godzilla* is that when people think of it, they immediately think of something that has nostalgic fun but is not to be taken seriously. For us, that posed an intriguing question: How do we reinvent *Godzilla* and bring it back to the way people felt when they sat in the movie theater and saw the very first one, for the very first time?" Devlin adds.

However, the filmmakers did not immediately warm up to the reptile. Lee confesses that he

"kept haranguing" his old friends about the project, visiting the set of *Independence Day* during the shoot to entreat them to take on *Godzilla*.

"We passed four times," Emmerich recalls. "I just wasn't sure it could be done without being kitschy. I heard about the project from Chris Lee and he mentioned it to me several times. I always said, 'Look, I'm working on something else, so not right now.' But, I always thought, how could we remake that? I had no clue. Then I heard that Jan was doing it and I thought, oh, Jan's a clever guy, that's good. He started

■ ABOVE LEFT: *Nick and Godzilla face to face.*
■ ABOVE RIGHT: *Godzilla's foot coming down on Animal.*
■ INSET: *Emmerich framed in broken-off tunnel.*

# THINK THEY DO THESE KIND OF MOVIES REALLY WELL BECAUSE THEY HAVE THEIR FINGER ON THE PULSE OF THE PUBLIC.

working on it. Then, all of a sudden, he was off the project and doing something else. So, Chris came to us again and said, 'So, why are you not doing this?' "

"The more I thought about it, the more I realized how fascinating it could be," Emmerich says. "At some point, Dean and I began to talk more seriously about it.

One day, we actually had the idea of how to do it but it was completely different from what they had. We really liked their script, but it had two creatures and there was a totally different feel to it. So, we approached the studio and said, 'We would like to rewrite everything. Would you consider that?' They said yes, but then there was this tumult at Sony."

The "tumult" resulted in the establishment of an entirely new regime, headed by former United Artists chief and erstwhile filmmaker John Calley. As the new president of Sony Pictures Entertainment one of Calley's first meetings was with Emmerich and Devlin.

Calley says, "I have great admiration for Dean and Roland. The idea of doing Godzilla with them and the possibilities that that represented seemed irresistible. Our relationship with them is extraordinary. They are real creators and managers of films and in addition to their talents as filmmakers, they are integrally involved in conceiving and supporting the marketing and merchandising (of the movie). They are true partners in every sense. It's thrilling to be associated with them.

"The Godzilla concept seems to have a mythic power that catches everyone's imagination. It seems to resonate in people, in a profound and universal way."

One daunting obstacle remained. Toho Co. Ltd., the creature's protective creators, had to agree to Emmerich and Devlin's new vision of *Godzilla*.

"I told TriStar, 'Guys, I don't think they're going to let us do this movie,' because I'd heard that Jan had some major, major problems when he wanted to change Godzilla. Our whole concept was totally based on changing Godzilla!"

This radical transformation began as a sketch by Patrick Tatopoulos. A veteran of several Emmerich/Devlin films, the French-born Tatopoulos last worked on the duo's *Independence Day*, for which he created the infamous alien invaders. Tatopoulos brought four sketches to Emmerich and Devlin in Cannes, where the filmmakers were

■ **ABOVE:** *Egg cracking in opening sequence.*

■ **LEFT:** *Godzilla's foot about to crush a crowd of people.*

■ **BELOW LEFT TO RIGHT:** *(a), (b) & (c) Pre-production paintings of the opening seuence of the movie. d) Painting showing Godzilla's strength and flexibility as he digs into an underwater pipe outlet.*

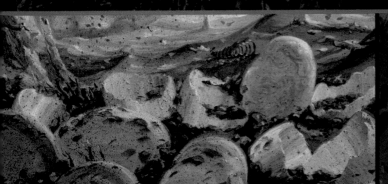

promoting *Independence Day*. The intensive publicity tour, on the heels of the film's grueling post-production schedule all conspired to drain Emmerich and Devlin's interest in immediately beginning another "event" picture. This was the mood Tatopoulos encountered when he arrived with his sketches of the new Godzilla. Fortunately, they proved to be the tonic required to reinvigorate Emmerich and Devlin's enthusiasm for *Godzilla*.

"They told me that when they took a look at the drawings, they suddenly got a new vision about the film and the sketches made them believe that, yeah, it could work. It's great to feel that I was a part of that in some way," Tatopoulos adds. In fact, the filmmakers acknowledged their debt to Tatopoulos by naming Matthew Broderick's character after him.

"We had a very talented designer in Patrick and I thought he nailed it on the first try," Emmerich says. "I never wanted to change it. The first impression is always the most important one."

Emmerich commissioned Tatopoulos to create a maquette based on the sketch he liked best, gambling that the new creature would also work its magic on Toho.

To that end, Emmerich, Tatopoulos, and Sony executives flew to Japan to meet with the Toho representatives to present their concept of the movie to Godzilla's creators. Devlin, unfortunately, could not join them. A stomach ailment leveled him in Germany, where he and Emmerich had been talking to the press

■ **LEFT:** *Godzilla is caught in crossing beams of light.*

■ **INSET LEFT:** *Dean Devlin dealing with urgent business while on the set.*

■ **RIGHT:** *Technicians prepare a large-scale Godzilla model for action.*

ONE DAY, WE ACTUALLY HAD THE IDEA OF HOW TO DO IT BUT

BUT IT WAS COMPLETELY DIFFERENT FROM WHAT THEY HAD.

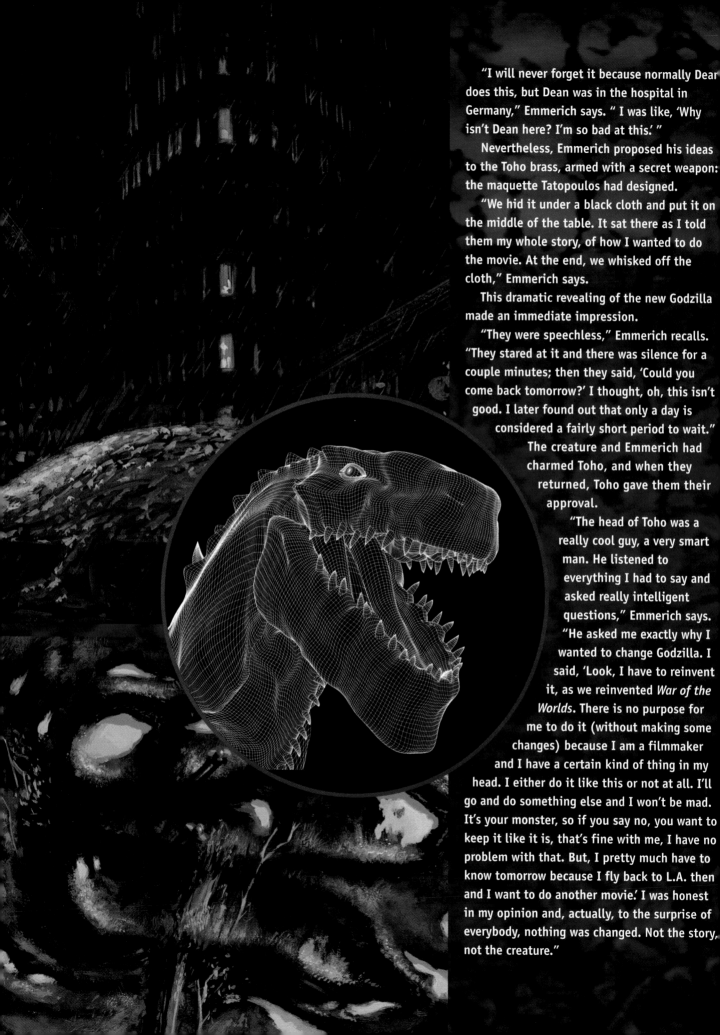

"I will never forget it because normally Dean does this, but Dean was in the hospital in Germany," Emmerich says. " I was like, 'Why isn't Dean here? I'm so bad at this.' "

Nevertheless, Emmerich proposed his ideas to the Toho brass, armed with a secret weapon: the maquette Tatopoulos had designed.

"We hid it under a black cloth and put it on the middle of the table. It sat there as I told them my whole story, of how I wanted to do the movie. At the end, we whisked off the cloth," Emmerich says.

This dramatic revealing of the new Godzilla made an immediate impression.

"They were speechless," Emmerich recalls. "They stared at it and there was silence for a couple minutes; then they said, 'Could you come back tomorrow?' I thought, oh, this isn't good. I later found out that only a day is considered a fairly short period to wait."

The creature and Emmerich had charmed Toho, and when they returned, Toho gave them their approval.

"The head of Toho was a really cool guy, a very smart man. He listened to everything I had to say and asked really intelligent questions," Emmerich says. "He asked me exactly why I wanted to change Godzilla. I said, 'Look, I have to reinvent it, as we reinvented *War of the Worlds*. There is no purpose for me to do it (without making some changes) because I am a filmmaker and I have a certain kind of thing in my head. I either do it like this or not at all. I'll go and do something else and I won't be mad. It's your monster, so if you say no, you want to keep it like it is, that's fine with me, I have no problem with that. But, I pretty much have to know tomorrow because I fly back to L.A. then and I want to do another movie.' I was honest in my opinion and, actually, to the surprise of everybody, nothing was changed. Not the story, not the creature."

Introducing Emmerich and Devlin's new creature to contemporary audiences fell to TriStar's marketing team, headed by Robert Levin, President, Worldwide Marketing.

"This movie needed to start production early, so that we knew we were going to have the movie for the summer of 1998, in early 1997. With Jeff Blake, President, Sony Pictures Releasing, and Roland and Dean, we determined that we ought to not just declare that we were coming out in the summer but actually to commit early to a release date.

"By doing so, we put ourselves in the enviable position of having a noncompetitive window of opportunity that doesn't come along very often with the number of movies being released these days. This was made possible because people believed in the potential of Godzilla, believed in the power of these two filmmakers to present something special. Everyone moved aside and said, 'We're not going up against that.' "

At first, Levin admits, the filmmakers threw him and his department "an unexpected curveball."

"I think that Dean and Roland are more attuned to what the marketing of a film represents to its success than any filmmakers I've ever worked with.

"In the beginning, we got indications from them that they really didn't think that the full figure Godzilla should be at all exposed prior to the release of the film. While initially we reacted negatively to that, once we understood their thinking behind it, it became completely acceptable to us.

"It took away from us the ability to do the obvious and created a challenge for us to do the remarkable sorts of things that I think we've been able to accomplish within the campaign. I think what we've discovered is that the power of imagination is more powerful than what you actually show people."

With Toho's blessing, the filmmakers set about creating a new monster, a contemporary incarnation of the original. Devlin describes the new Godzilla as " more ferocious and spectacular and surprising than his predecessors. Lethal, fast, and agile, a definite monster."

---

■ UPPER LEFT: *Floodlights illuminating the fishpile near the Flatiron Building.*

■ LOWER LEFT: *Pre-production of people standing in the giant footprint.*

■ INSET: *A CG wireframe rendering of Godzilla's head.*

■ RIGHT: *The "man-in-the-suit"" technique was used when Godzilla breaks out of a 1/24th scale street in front of Matthew Broderick who will be inserted in the shot via digital compositing.*

However, the movie will also pay homage to the creature that terrorized Tokyo in the mid-fifties.

"We wanted to stay true to the essence of why Godzilla was created in the first place, which had to do with a lot of people's fears of what was going on with weapons and radiation. You have to remember how the first Godzilla was created. The original was made in Japan shortly after World War II, and the devastation caused by the two nuclear bombs was obviously on the minds of the Japanese people. So, we kept that theme going. We really wanted to honor where it came from and yet start anew."

Devlin adds that he and Emmerich approached their Godzilla as if it was an entirely new creation.

Devlin saw his first *Godzilla* film as a youth and his affection for the franchise comes from his childhood.

"Growing up in Los Angeles, on Sunday afternoons, they would show all the old *Godzilla* movies and immediately after, they'd have all the *Star Trek* episodes, so that's how I spent my Sundays," he recalls.

Emmerich observes that the Japanese *Godzilla* films owe much to the great stop-animation artist Ray Harryhausen, one of Emmerich's favorite filmmakers.

"There is an American movie called *The Beast from 2000 Fathoms*, shot in the early fifties (1953). This movie was done with stop-animation and it was one of Ray Harryhausen's best work. There was a big dinosaur resurrected or awakened by an atomic blast. It swims around and ends up in New York and the last final scene is at Coney Island. Obviously, the Japanese saw that movie and said, oh, we should do something like that, too. But they had no clue how to do stop-animation. It was a pretty sophisticated thing and actually Ray Harryhausen was the absolute master."

■ LEFT: *Concept painting of a view through destroyed subway station to a tunnel dug by Godzilla.*

■ RIGHT INSET: *View of nest in Madison Square Garden with entry hole in center.*

■ RIGHT: *Painting of survivor in water watching destruction of giant fish-factory ship (wider angle).*

Emmerich says that while he enjoyed the classic *Godzilla* films, he did not want to recreate them.

"I didn't want to remake the original *Godzilla*. We took part of the basic storyline, in that the creature is created by radiation and it becomes a big challenge. But that's all we took. Then we thought, what would we do today with a monster movie and a story like that. We forgot everything about the original *Godzilla* right there.

"We had to ask ourselves, what is scary and what is new? It becomes frightening because he is an animal that disturbs the life of a busy city. Godzilla behaves like a trapped animal trying to survive and the scariness comes from the sheer fact that you have to deal with a huge animal that is unpredictable. He's doing what he has to do. In a way, he is created by us, in that we influence nature, we create something that doesn't exist in nature and nature strikes back. The 'new' I left to Patrick Tatopoulos," Emmerich explains.

To differentiate between the original Japanese *Godzilla* and the TriStar version, Toho resolved to refer to their monster as the "Classic Godzilla," while his contemporary cousin would be the "New Godzilla." His updated look was due in part to the advances in technology that obviated the need for the man-in-the-suit who typically brought Classic Godzilla to life.

"It's actually a pretty obvious thing. We are living in a time where people have seen *Jurassic Park* and *The Lost World* and we don't have the same kind of limitations the Japanese had when they made their *Godzilla*," Emmerich comments. "They said, 'Why don't we put a man in a suit?' So, they built a big rubber suit but a rubber suit was much bulkier, because if it was too close to the human body, it gave away that there was a person inside it. It had these big, fat legs and couldn't walk very fast. It developed this kind of 'Godzilla walk.' Now, with the new effects technology, we don't have that limitation and it slims down the creature enormously."

Unfettered by Classic Godzilla's awkward movements, Emmerich and Devlin could concoct a storyline around a feral, lithe, quick predator. They discussed the new creature with Tatopoulos and all agreed that he would look toward nature when designing the monster.

"Roland's idea was to make a very fast creature, there was no way I could use the old design and make it fast," Tatopoulos remembers. "Roland really encouraged me to come up with something unique and said, 'Don't get tied up

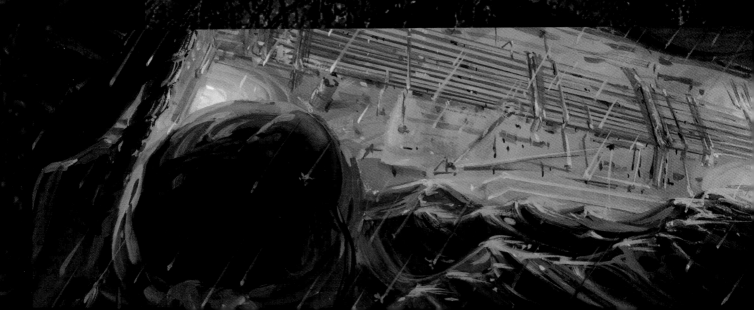

with the old design, let's just go crazy.' It became a very easy job because it was like, oh, great, something completely new. The only challenge was not to make this creature look like a T-Rex or a gigantic dinosaur because we've seen this in *Jurassic Park* and even more in *The Lost World* where the T-Rex runs through the street. At that time, we didn't know about it (because *The Lost World* hadn't opened yet) but fortunately, this guy doesn't look like a dinosaur. It is a dragon more than anything else. A dragon with textures and a finish that is very realistic, so that we feel, oh, it is real dragon, it is alive. Roland really wanted this character not to be an unbelievable monster but at the same time we didn't want to make a realistic dinosaur either, so that's where the challenge was."

Much of the creature's look began to evolve in Japan, after Toho had approved the maquette.

"We had some downtime between showing the stuff to the people at Toho and at that point we really started to develop the character, talking many late evenings, trying to decide what it would be doing . . . we couldn't stop talking about the thing. All that stuff, the speed, the look, the attitude of the character, the way it would react, the fact that it would act more like a lizard but have aspects of other reptiles, all that was determined at that point," Tatopoulos explains.

Ultimately, Tatopoulos endowed his Godzilla with the characteristics of many animals and the end result is an amalgamation of a variety of species.

"The original concept was that he would look like a lizard or crocodile. We looked at books on dinosaurs, crocodiles, reptiles. From them and from reference tapes, we got suggestions of textures, colors, and movement . . . movement was from studying iguanas, things we can relate to. Even horses with the muscle motion, for the muscle in the legs. I also wanted to make a creature that had human features, so the torso and the arms are also somewhat human, even though he doesn't really grab things; he uses his mouth. The tail is like a gigantic crocodile's, the head has crocodile features as well, so it is a realistic creature, in some ways," Tatopoulos says.

Tatopoulos was also inspired by the ferocious, feline grace and danger of big cats, such as lions and tigers. In fact, one famous tiger served as his archetype.

"I did some tweaking, to give it something different. I gave him a chin. It gives him a lot of nobility. My inspiration was a tiger. For the old Godzilla, they used a dog as the inspiration. If you look at the old Godzilla, it has the nose of a dog, the muscles of a dog's face and those tiny little ears. I felt we should use an animal in that style but make it look like a reptile, but I used the tiger. One of the inspirations was a character I really loved as a kid, the tiger in *Jungle Book*, Shere Khan. He had this great chin thing and I always loved it, he looked scary, evil, but you respected him. I thought, let's try to give him a chin and I felt it still looked realistic but he had this different thing that you hadn't seen before."

While Godzilla's chin was born of a tiger, he owed his mutable, subtle hues to the dragon family, a real one, owned by Patrick Tatopoulos. A longtime admirer of all things reptile, Tatopoulos always visits the local paleontology

■ BELOW: *Storyboard sequence showing discovery of the nest and Audrey's surprise and terror as Baby Godzillas begin to emerge.*

■ LEFT: *Godzilla turns to look back (Chrysler Building in background).*

■ RIGHT: *(a) eggs on tiers of seats. (b) & (c) two views of Madison Square Garden nests. (d) Babies in front of Madison Square Garden escalators.*

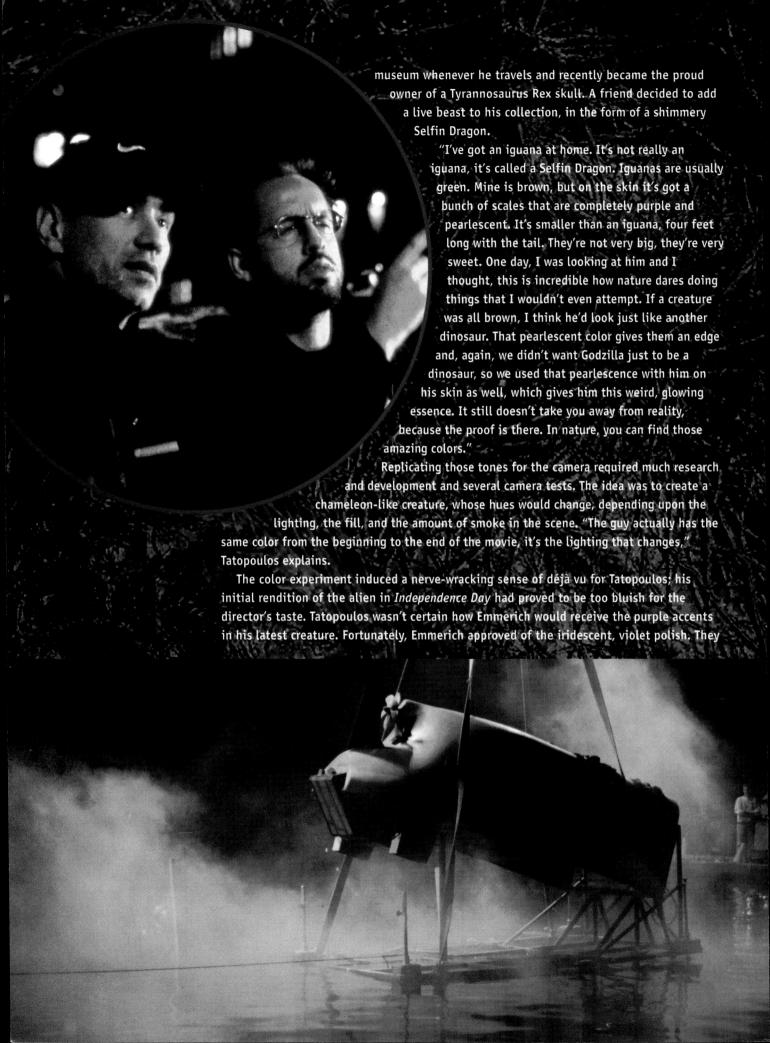

museum whenever he travels and recently became the proud owner of a Tyrannosaurus Rex skull. A friend decided to add a live beast to his collection, in the form of a shimmery Selfin Dragon.

"I've got an iguana at home. It's not really an iguana, it's called a Selfin Dragon. Iguanas are usually green. Mine is brown, but on the skin it's got a bunch of scales that are completely purple and pearlescent. It's smaller than an iguana, four feet long with the tail. They're not very big, they're very sweet. One day, I was looking at him and I thought, this is incredible how nature dares doing things that I wouldn't even attempt. If a creature was all brown, I think he'd look just like another dinosaur. That pearlescent color gives them an edge and, again, we didn't want Godzilla just to be a dinosaur, so we used that pearlescence with him on his skin as well, which gives him this weird, glowing essence. It still doesn't take you away from reality, because the proof is there. In nature, you can find those amazing colors."

Replicating those tones for the camera required much research and development and several camera tests. The idea was to create a chameleon-like creature, whose hues would change, depending upon the lighting, the fill, and the amount of smoke in the scene. "The guy actually has the same color from the beginning to the end of the movie, it's the lighting that changes," Tatopoulos explains.

The color experiment induced a nerve-wracking sense of déjà vu for Tatopoulos; his initial rendition of the alien in *Independence Day* had proved to be too bluish for the director's taste. Tatopoulos wasn't certain how Emmerich would receive the purple accents in his latest creature. Fortunately, Emmerich approved of the iridescent, violet polish. They learned that the painters needed to add more layers of shiny paint for it to read on camera properly.

"We had to load them with the pearlescent color because the camera doesn't catch as much as we do with the real eye. We noticed when we did the color camera test that it was extremely pearlescent, but we looked at it on camera and we'd lost

about fifty percent of the pearlescence. So, when you look at it like that, you see twice as much as you're going to read on camera."

Because Godzilla is so huge, (Devlin customarily measured him as "twenty-stories-high,") it was impossible to affect these camera tests on him. Fortunately, "he" had a litter of ravenous babies in the script. Like some amphibians and certainly like several species adapting to human-induced toxins, Godzilla is both male and female and reproduces asexually. This transgenderism earned him different monikers among the crews laboring to bring him to life. Tatopoulos's creature effects team referred to him as "Mom," the shooting crew used variations of the pronoun "him," and the visual effects unit adopted the code name "Fred."

"Team Fred," as the visual effects folk came to call themselves, was headed by Visual Effects Producer Volker Engel, who served in the same capacity on *Independence Day* and won an Academy Award for his efforts. For Engel, the biggest challenge of *Godzilla* was the film's star. Creating the creature that Emmerich and Devlin had envisioned proved to be much more complicated than anything he'd experienced on *Independence Day*.

"Everything evolved around the creature," Engel observes. "It was a really different experience than *Independence Day* where we dealt with thousands of model components that had to be put together to create the final images. In this movie the creature is the centerpiece. We have Matthew Broderick and Jean Reno, and an overall terrific cast, but the movie is still called *Godzilla*. It is a living, breathing animal, Every piece of destruction had to look like it was done by a real creature. So, we knew from the beginning: if we should fail to establish him as a living animal, the whole movie wouldn't work. That was the single biggest challenge.

"I sometimes called him the Jim Carrey of our movie. He was pretty expensive and if he didn't carry the movie, we were in big trouble."

■ ABOVE: *For an early shoot to test materials for "crash-through" sequences, a Godzilla head on a stick is being rammed through miniature walls consisting of different materials.*

■ LEFT INSET: *Emmerich and Engel planning night scene.*

■ OPPOSITE PAGE BOTTOM: *Fish-factory ship model being lowered into place for destruction sequence.*

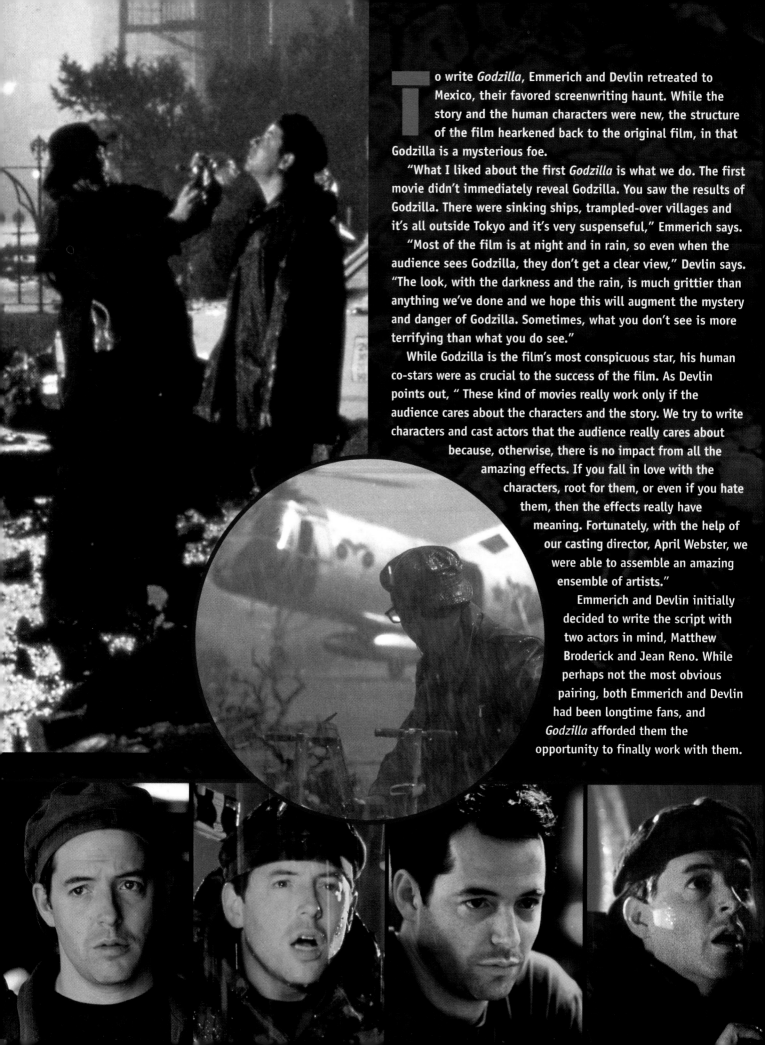

To write *Godzilla*, Emmerich and Devlin retreated to Mexico, their favored screenwriting haunt. While the story and the human characters were new, the structure of the film hearkened back to the original film, in that Godzilla is a mysterious foe.

"What I liked about the first *Godzilla* is what we do. The first movie didn't immediately reveal Godzilla. You saw the results of Godzilla. There were sinking ships, trampled-over villages and it's all outside Tokyo and it's very suspenseful," Emmerich says.

"Most of the film is at night and in rain, so even when the audience sees Godzilla, they don't get a clear view," Devlin says. "The look, with the darkness and the rain, is much grittier than anything we've done and we hope this will augment the mystery and danger of Godzilla. Sometimes, what you don't see is more terrifying than what you do see."

While Godzilla is the film's most conspicuous star, his human co-stars were as crucial to the success of the film. As Devlin points out, " These kind of movies really work only if the audience cares about the characters and the story. We try to write characters and cast actors that the audience really cares about because, otherwise, there is no impact from all the amazing effects. If you fall in love with the characters, root for them, or even if you hate them, then the effects really have meaning. Fortunately, with the help of our casting director, April Webster, we were able to assemble an amazing ensemble of artists."

Emmerich and Devlin initially decided to write the script with two actors in mind, Matthew Broderick and Jean Reno. While perhaps not the most obvious pairing, both Emmerich and Devlin had been longtime fans, and *Godzilla* afforded them the opportunity to finally work with them.

"Ever since Roland and I started working together, we have wanted to work with Matthew Broderick. He's one of our favorite actors in the world and it's never worked out. Finally, we were in a position where we could make a movie together and it has been a lot of fun. He brought a lot of humor to the part and really got the spirit of the movie," Devlin says.

Emmerich laughs. "You know, I always wanted to work with Matthew. This is actually embarrassing, but I wanted to cast him in so many movies and it was always something. This time we said, 'We'll change it around. We'll go first to Matthew.' So, we did. We told him, 'We'll write a script and you will be in it and you will be that part. Because the script will be there in six weeks and it's your part if you want it.' He read it and he wanted to do it. That was the safest possible route to get Matthew Broderick. There's one little homage to Ferris Bueller which is actually really funny. It has to do with an elevator."

Indeed, Broderick accepted the part of the "worm guy," a scientist studying the effects of radiation on the Chernobyl earthworm. In fact, his character is inspired by actual scientists that Devlin read about and so the "worm guy" was born.

Devlin says that they'd admired Jean Reno's work "ever since *The Big Blue*, on through *La Femme Nikita* and *The Professional*. As with Matthew Broderick, we wrote the part for him. When we started writing the script, we thought, who gets most upset when buildings are destroyed? Well, the insurance companies do. So, we thought it would be interesting to have this French insurance investigator trying to find out the cause of all this damage. We immediately thought of Jean Reno."

"I saw him in *The Big Blue* and I thought, wow, what a guy! Then I saw him in *The Professional* and I wanted to do something with him," Emmerich says. "Actually, it was like this. We were writing this part for Matthew and we said who could be a great counterpart for Matthew? Then we said . . . Jean Reno! It was just like that because we had roughly a story . . . and he agreed to do it but he had to do *Les Visateurs II* and he thought he could postpone it, but he couldn't, so we had to work around that shooting schedule. We told him what we wanted to do with him, he was really excited because he loved *Godzilla* as a kid, and then we sent him the script when it was finished and not even one word was changed."

"It was a unique opportunity for us because we were writing the script and dreaming the parts *and* we actually got the very people we had in mind, which was exciting," Devlin says.

■ FAR LEFT: *Lighting check on Broderick.*

■ LEFT INSET: *Dr. Nick Tatopoulos is about to be interrupted during his research.*

■ BELOW LEFT TO RIGHT: *A range of views of Matthew Broderick through the course of the film.*

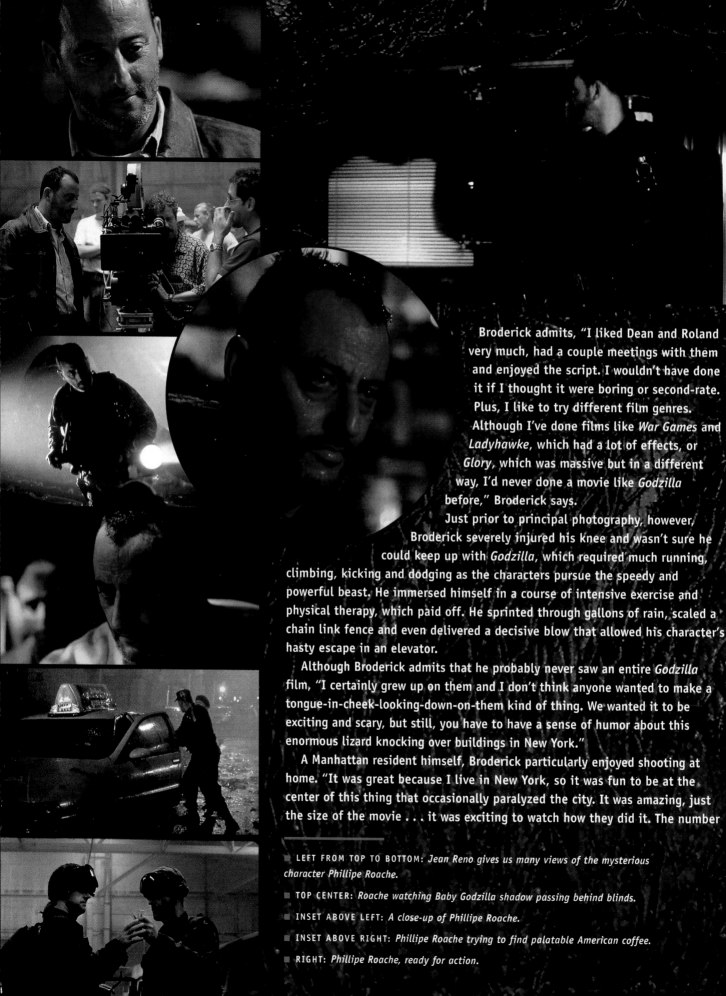

Broderick admits, "I liked Dean and Roland very much, had a couple meetings with them and enjoyed the script. I wouldn't have done it if I thought it were boring or second-rate. Plus, I like to try different film genres. Although I've done films like *War Games* and *Ladyhawke*, which had a lot of effects, or *Glory*, which was massive but in a different way, I'd never done a movie like *Godzilla* before," Broderick says.

Just prior to principal photography, however, Broderick severely injured his knee and wasn't sure he could keep up with *Godzilla*, which required much running, climbing, kicking and dodging as the characters pursue the speedy and powerful beast. He immersed himself in a course of intensive exercise and physical therapy, which paid off. He sprinted through gallons of rain, scaled a chain link fence and even delivered a decisive blow that allowed his character's hasty escape in an elevator.

Although Broderick admits that he probably never saw an entire *Godzilla* film, "I certainly grew up on them and I don't think anyone wanted to make a tongue-in-cheek-looking-down-on-them kind of thing. We wanted it to be exciting and scary, but still, you have to have a sense of humor about this enormous lizard knocking over buildings in New York."

A Manhattan resident himself, Broderick particularly enjoyed shooting at home. "It was great because I live in New York, so it was fun to be at the center of this thing that occasionally paralyzed the city. It was amazing, just the size of the movie . . . it was exciting to watch how they did it. The number

■ LEFT FROM TOP TO BOTTOM: *Jean Reno gives us many views of the mysterious character Phillipe Roache.*

■ TOP CENTER: *Roache watching Baby Godzilla shadow passing behind blinds.*

■ INSET ABOVE LEFT: *A close-up of Phillipe Roache.*

■ INSET ABOVE RIGHT: *Phillipe Roache trying to find palatable American coffee.*

■ RIGHT: *Phillipe Roache, ready for action.*

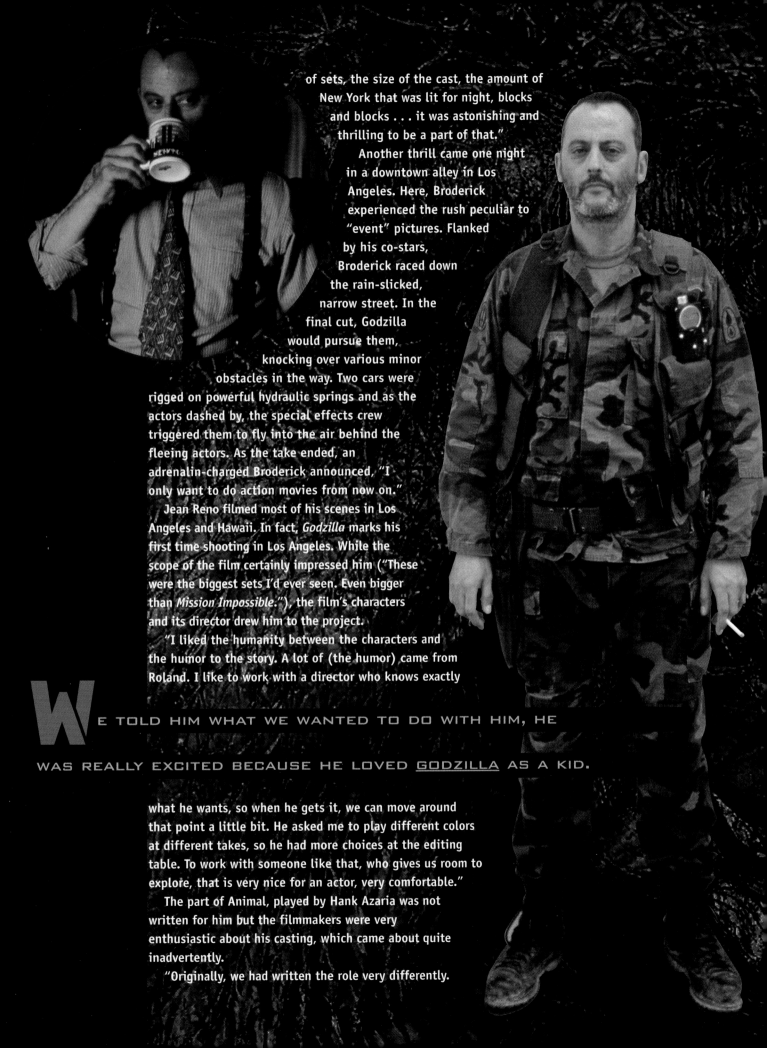

of sets, the size of the cast, the amount of New York that was lit for night, blocks and blocks . . . it was astonishing and thrilling to be a part of that."

Another thrill came one night in a downtown alley in Los Angeles. Here, Broderick experienced the rush peculiar to "event" pictures. Flanked by his co-stars, Broderick raced down the rain-slicked, narrow street. In the final cut, Godzilla would pursue them, knocking over various minor obstacles in the way. Two cars were rigged on powerful hydraulic springs and as the actors dashed by, the special effects crew triggered them to fly into the air behind the fleeing actors. As the take ended, an adrenalin-charged Broderick announced, "I only want to do action movies from now on."

Jean Reno filmed most of his scenes in Los Angeles and Hawaii. In fact, *Godzilla* marks his first time shooting in Los Angeles. While the scope of the film certainly impressed him ("These were the biggest sets I'd ever seen. Even bigger than *Mission Impossible*."), the film's characters and its director drew him to the project.

"I liked the humanity between the characters and the humor to the story. A lot of (the humor) came from Roland. I like to work with a director who knows exactly

WE TOLD HIM WHAT WE WANTED TO DO WITH HIM, HE WAS REALLY EXCITED BECAUSE HE LOVED <u>GODZILLA</u> AS A KID.

what he wants, so when he gets it, we can move around that point a little bit. He asked me to play different colors at different takes, so he had more choices at the editing table. To work with someone like that, who gives us room to explore, that is very nice for an actor, very comfortable."

The part of Animal, played by Hank Azaria was not written for him but the filmmakers were very enthusiastic about his casting, which came about quite inadvertently.

"Originally, we had written the role very differently.

I actually ran into Hank Azaria at a restaurant. We started talking and I realized that this is a guy who does really incredible characters and every part he plays is totally different. I talked it over with Roland and he liked the idea of an actor who could create something completely different from what we had in mind. When we met with him, we immediately felt that this was a guy who could bring a whole lot more to the role. He's just a wonderful, wonderful actor who comes to the project with an enormous amount of energy and love for *Godzilla*, because he is a *Godzilla* fan from way back," Devlin says.

"It's true. The *Godzilla* movies were on every Saturday morning in New York, where I grew up," Azaria says. "When *Godzilla vs. King Kong* came out, that was a big deal when I was growing up. I remember actively worrying about who would win."

Of all the characters in the film trying to snare Godzilla, Azaria's Animal adopts probably the most reckless approach.

Occasionally, Animal's daring led to painful moments for the actor playing him.

"My character is a very New York, Italian, sarcastic cameraman. He's a guy who will do whatever it takes to get the shot, he's running around, trying to photograph Godzilla. Of course, most people are running away from Godzilla, but I'm running toward him. The hundreds of extras were running from Godzilla, looking behind them as I was running forward. I was constantly smashed by all the extras running forward and looking back. I almost died many times. One of the extras really barreled into me as he was running away. I got banged pretty nicely in the face."

Azaria later proved to have more impressive coordination. Under the guidance of Stunt Coordinator R.A. Rondell, he literally overcame an Emmerich-devised New York

■ TOP LEFT: *Audrey and Animal in the newsroom.*

■ TOP CENTER: *Audrey showing her brightly colored raincoat.*

■ TOP RIGHT: *Animal jamming tape into camera.*

■ LEFT INSET: *Lucy close-up on subway.*

■ RIGHT INSET: *Audrey in a moment of surprise.*

■ FAR RIGHT FROM TOP TO BOTTOM: *(a) Animal in his apartment, surrounded by refugees from Godzilla rampage. (b) Animal persuades Audrey to go after her story. (c) Audrey's office preparing for evacuation. (d) Model for Godzilla's toes being lowered toward Animal. (e) Animal smashes open doors on the overturned van to get a video camera so he can pursue Godzilla.*

traffic jam by bounding over the cars, video camera perched on his shoulder, as Animal tries to photograph the elusive Godzilla.

Azaria figured Animal got his name because "he's sort of reckless and nuts and doesn't care about his own safety." He came to understand that there was an additional rationale for the moniker. While shooting a pivotal scene in Los Angeles when Godzilla ambles by a diner in which Animal and his friend Audrey and his wife, Lucy, are lunching, Azaria stuffed a hefty hamburger down his gullet, take after take. Soon, he was also chugging Alka-Seltzer in between setups. "Then I realized he was also called Animal because he eats like a pig," Azaria says.

Fortunately, Azaria was blessed with a strong stomach. He also discovered that he possessed an added skill, which helped him follow, photograph and otherwise react to a giant, if invisible, monster. A longtime member of the animated series *The Simpsons*, Azaria had ample experience acting with imaginary co-stars.

"For some of the actors, it was a little weird, acting to nothing, but it wasn't for me. I wondered why wasn't this a problem for me, but I realized that on *The Simpsons*, that's all we do, we're always screaming and yelling and being frightened of nothing. It seemed normal to me.

"Most of the time, we had a lot of production assistants walking around with X's for eyeline purposes, people on megaphones announcing what Godzilla was doing. That got a little silly. 'And he's ANGRY. And he's WALKING.' We started making stuff up, like 'We're not sure WHAT he's doing, he's HARD to read. Now he's CRYING. Now he's impressed with your NECKTIE,'" Azaria recalls.

Animal's colleague Audrey is played by Maria Pitillo. The filmmakers have a history of casting their female leads at the last possible second. While Pitillo came to the picture in a more timely fashion, it still took a while to find her.

"We had done an exhaustive search to find the right woman to play Audrey. It was very hard because there are a lot of different sides to this character. She's adorable and sweet but she's also ambitious and professional. There must be something about her so that when you meet her, you

understand that she's inexperienced but she ends up surprising you with her capability. Maria came in and just blew us away. She brought the character a real effervescence, but when she needs to, she can also become a very tough reporter," Devlin comments.

"Maria won me over with her comic timing. It was great," Emmerich says. "She had to have good chemistry with Matthew but she also had to be together a lot with Hank Azaria who is very quick and funny, so she had to keep up with him too."

It's no coincidence that Azaria's gonzo cameraman Animal and Pitillo's Audrey are friends, because they are both ambitious journalists. However, his particular zeal alarms as much as it inspires her.

"She's striving to get ahead in journalism, to prove herself. She will do anything to get the story, which, in this case, is Godzilla. Animal is the same way but his name says it all. He just goes for it and drags her along, even to places she doesn't want to go," Pitillo remarks.

She found Emmelrich very helpful in terms of honing the character as the movie progressed.

"I think Roland and I connected early on, I think we saw Audrey the same way and he would encourage me to come up with things as we shot. He'd give me little notes and ideas and we sort of shaped her together. We found little things that made her more funny."

Pitillo adds that Roland's sanguine disposition also made for a happy shooting experience, no mean feat as the movie filmed for five months, in several locations, mostly from sunset to sunrise, in a steady Emmerich-made downpour. Despite the cold, wet, long hours, very few of the cast and crew complained and attributed the general good cheer to Emmerich and Devlin's joie de vivre.

"Roland and Dean were always having a good time, we could tell. They always kept their sense of humor. I mean, they were tired sometimes, we all got tired, but they kept the fun going," Pitillo says.

Emmerich also conscientiously explained the effects to the cast, so the actors could see how the final scene would look. This was

■ ABOVE FROM LEFT TO RIGHT: *(a) Craven and Chapman celebrate victory. (b) Craven in the midst of action. (c) Chapman is deep in research. (d) Charles Caiman is coming on strong to Audrey. (e) A blue-screen shot of Charles Caiman and his broadcasting partner on the air.*

■ LEFT: *Lucy (Arabella Field) in refugee party scene.*

■ BELOW: *Another view of Lucy.*

■ RIGHT: *Dr. Elsie Chapman (Vicki Lewis).*

Charles Caiman
the name you
trust in news

particularly helpful when the actors had to shoot a scene several times, to accommodate their giant unseen nemesis, Godzilla. For example, a scene in which Broderick, Azaria, Reno, and Pitillo ran down an alley to escape Godzilla was shot on location in downtown Los Angeles and back on stage at Sony, against green screen for later addition of background and effects.

Harry Shearer, who plays Charles Caiman, a pompous television reporter, with a suspiciously familiar broadcast style, says that Emmerich's enthusiasm was infectious and made for a festive, warm atmosphere.

"We shot in New York in the beginning of May and it was thirty-six degrees at night. It was about two-thirty in the morning, we were making rain. After we finished the shot, they turned the rain machines off and we were standing there in, I swear, this white stuff. It was so cold that the residual rain lingering in the air had turned to snow. But, I must say it was fun because Roland was having the time of his life. He was just great. Even in the midst of these weather agonies. I just think it's the way he's wired, he just had a great time and sort of swept us along in the flow of it."

Shearer's portrayal of Caiman aided Emmerich and Devlin's jolly mood. His ad-libs and sonorous malapropisms routinely sent Emmerich and Devlin into fits of laughter as they watched the scene unfold at the video monitor and again at dailies. As with several other *Godzilla* characters, Shearer's rendition of the character differed from the filmmakers' original vision.

Arabella Field plays Lucy, Animal's wife and Audrey's friend and colleague. Casting director April Webster suggested Field and Devlin says that "Arabella just had us on the floor laughing."

Field did not read with her on-screen husband Azaria during her audition but the pair had a good film rapport, since, coincidentally, they'd worked together on the CBS television show *If Not for You*.

The other key female role is Dr. Elsie Chapman, who collaborates with Nick Tatopoulos. Chapman, a blunt scientist whose brilliance, in part, compensates for a lack of social grace, is played by Vicki Lewis, who is probably best known for her weekly, wacky performances on the NBC series *NewsRadio*.

"Like the other actors, she brought so much to the part that we weren't expecting. We found that with her, we weren't so much laughing at the character as with her and that made it

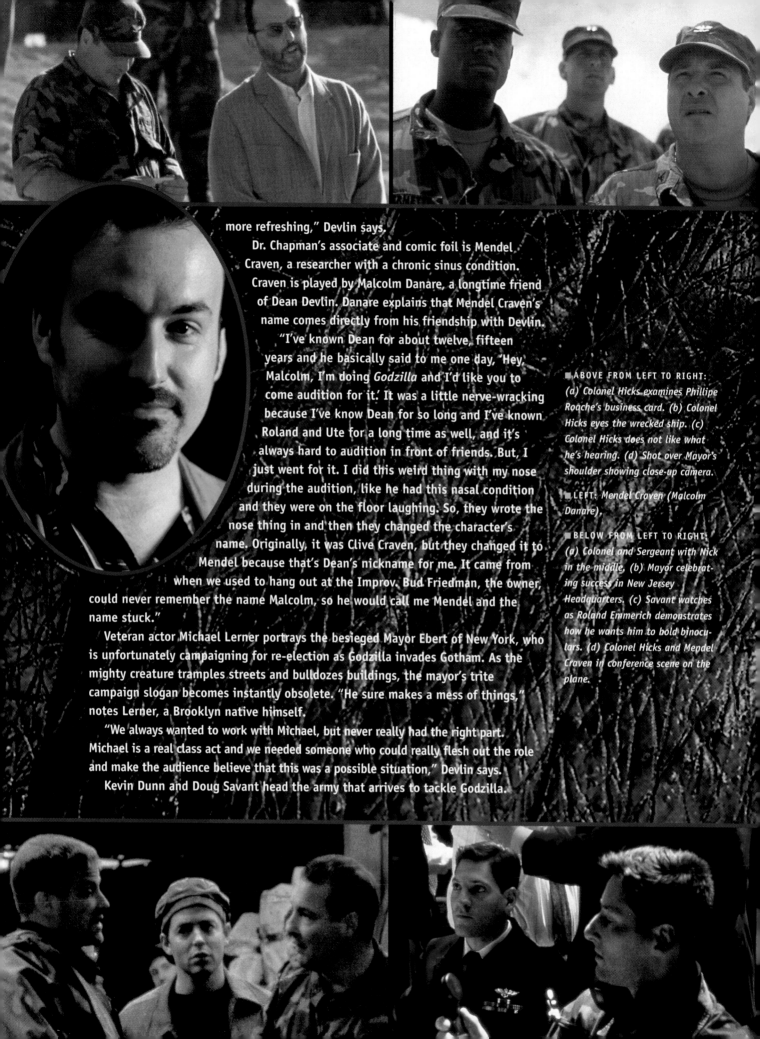

more refreshing," Devlin says.

Dr. Chapman's associate and comic foil is Mendel Craven, a researcher with a chronic sinus condition. Craven is played by Malcolm Danare, a longtime friend of Dean Devlin. Danare explains that Mendel Craven's name comes directly from his friendship with Devlin.

"I've known Dean for about twelve, fifteen years and he basically said to me one day, 'Hey, Malcolm, I'm doing *Godzilla* and I'd like you to come audition for it.' It was a little nerve-wracking because I've know Dean for so long and I've known Roland and Ute for a long time as well, and it's always hard to audition in front of friends. But, I just went for it. I did this weird thing with my nose during the audition, like he had this nasal condition and they were on the floor laughing. So, they wrote the nose thing in and then they changed the character's name. Originally, it was Clive Craven, but they changed it to Mendel because that's Dean's nickname for me. It came from when we used to hang out at the Improv. Bud Friedman, the owner, could never remember the name Malcolm, so he would call me Mendel and the name stuck."

Veteran actor Michael Lerner portrays the besieged Mayor Ebert of New York, who is unfortunately campaigning for re-election as Godzilla invades Gotham. As the mighty creature tramples streets and bulldozes buildings, the mayor's trite campaign slogan becomes instantly obsolete. "He sure makes a mess of things," notes Lerner, a Brooklyn native himself.

"We always wanted to work with Michael, but never really had the right part. Michael is a real class act and we needed someone who could really flesh out the role and make the audience believe that this was a possible situation," Devlin says.

Kevin Dunn and Doug Savant head the army that arrives to tackle Godzilla.

■ ABOVE FROM LEFT TO RIGHT: (a) Colonel Hicks examines Phillipe Roache's business card. (b) Colonel Hicks eyes the wrecked ship. (c) Colonel Hicks does not like what he's hearing. (d) Shot over Mayor's shoulder showing close-up camera.

■ LEFT: Mendel Craven (Malcolm Danare).

■ BELOW FROM LEFT TO RIGHT: (a) Colonel and Sergeant with Nick in the middle. (b) Mayor celebrating success in New Jersey Headquarters. (c) Savant watches as Roland Emmerich demonstrates how he wants him to bold binoculars. (d) Colonel Hicks and Mendel Craven in conference scene on the plane.

Although one might expect the military to rally if a giant beast decided to roam New York, the filmmakers did not want Colonel Hicks and Sergeant O'Neal, respectively, to be standard-issue characters.

"We didn't want the Colonel to be this typical shouting commander. We wanted someone who was almost immediately likable, so that you sympathize with this enormous problem he has on his hands. The way Kevin plays him, you immediately feel that this guy is under tremendous pressure, but also has that military reserve and an underlying humanity," Devlin explains.

Doug Savant, as Dunn's subordinate Sergeant O'Neal, came to the film as "an old poker-playing buddy of mine from years back and Roland's known him for a long time," Devlin says. "He came in with such an original take on this character that we ended up rewriting the part for him."

Savant's interpretation of Sergeant O'Neal makes for some unexpected and funny moments, as he tries to control the Godzilla-induced chaos with the help of his polar opposite, the decidedly unmilitary, inquisitive scientist Nick Tatopoulos.

"When I came into the audition, I just really saw the character in terms of the military. He only knows how to deal with things in terms of rank, so he never knew quite how Matthew's character fit in to that scheme. Nick's not someone O'Neal would

ANIMAL IS THE SAME WAY BUT HIS NAME SAYS IT ALL. HE JUST GOES

FOR IT AND DRAGS HER ALONG, EVEN TO PLACES SHE DOESN'T WANT TO GO.

necessarily respect, but he's the guy O'Neal needs for answers. O'Neal is just dying to have a way to control the situation and he's looking for reassurance from Nick, who constantly gives him none, so he's absolutely frustrated with Nick."

Savant says, "The fun of playing Sergeant O'Neal was that he is utterly out of his depth, completely in over his head. He is a professional military guy who deals with everything as a military man should, but this is Godzilla and traditional maneuvers just aren't going to work. He's in charge of all these troops, he's got half a dozen tanks, probably two hundred to three hundred men with rocket launchers and F–16s and grenades and guns and you know what? That's not enough to deal with Godzilla. O'Neal is overmatched."

While the film shot on various locations, beginning in New York and ending in Los Angeles, with a week in Hawaii, the story is set primarily in Manhattan. Only New York played itself; Los Angeles stages and locations doubled for Gotham, and Hawaii stood in for Tahiti, Jamaica, and Panama. Aside from a certain fondness the filmmakers harbor for Manhattan, there were practical reasons to set *Godzilla* there.

"We needed a location as big as Godzilla and, after Tokyo, only New York has that kind of scale and drama," notes Executive Producer Fay. Roland Emmerich adds, "There are certain cities and skylines you can cheat by using other locations, but New York is definitely not one of them. It's such a well-known, American landmark."

Not only did the buildings supply the proper proportions, the sinewy urban canyons and intricate hiding places offered by the city also seemed a perfect lair for an animal, even one the size of Godzilla.

"It's a magical town, it looks better than any other town, it has these urban canyons. It's perfect for a big animal to hide in, with its subways and the fact that it is an island, protected, surrounded by water. It had this nice perfect harbor, with the river . . . the perfect spot (in which) to settle down," Emmerich muses.

In April 1997, prior to the start of principal photography, the department heads of all the *Godzilla* shooting crew departments, from electric to production design, met for a production meeting. Chaired by Director Roland Emmerich and Executive Producer Bill Fay, the assembly took place on the Sony lot.

TriStar Production Executive Ray Zimmerman also attended the meeting. He

■ LEFT FROM TOP TO BOTTOM: *(a) Crowd outside New Jersey Headquarters as Godzilla team arrives. (b) Nick arriving at New Jersey Headquarters in the rain. (c) Monitoring action in New Jersey Headquarters. (d)Crowd watches action on monitor in New Jersey Headquarters. (e) Colonel Hicks on field phone.*

■ ABOVE INSET: *Emmerich directing rain scene at New Jersey Headquarters*

■ UPPER RIGHT FROM LEFT TO RIGHT: *Pre-production paintings: (a) Idea for Military Camp. (b) The International Conference Room. (c) Main Tent Entrance.*

■ FAR RIGHT FROM TOP TO BOTTOM: *(a) Celebrating victory in headquarters. (b) A hallway in the New Jersey Military Headquarters. (c) Military team monitoring activity.*

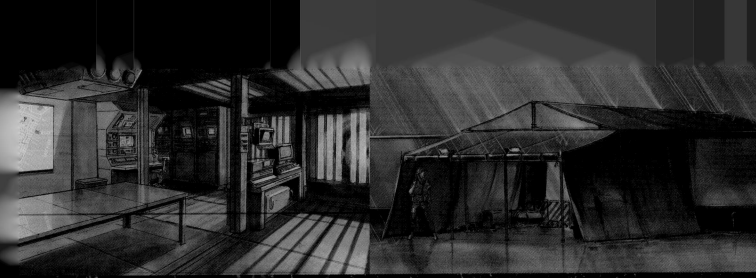

greeted the crew and announced enthusiastically, "This is the biggest movie we've ever made at this studio."

The subsequent shooting schedule proved him right. Principal photography began in New York, in May 1997 and ended in Los Angeles four months later. Everything about the shoot was literally of Godzillian proportions. The final crew list was 164 pages long and its table of contents subdivided into four units. This tome didn't even include the nine page index of visual effects members nor the two sheets detailing the creature shop artists.

The first day of shooting offered the cast and crew an example of the giant adventure they were about to begin. Filming just outside New York, in Jersey City, New Jersey, required 150 extras, three military sedans, two military forklifts, three newsvans, twenty-five military vehicles, from Humvees to Jeeps, one mock missile launcher, two New Jersey police cars, three tanks, two searchlights, two black sedans and one satellite dish truck. And rain, oceans of it. It poured from the sky and from two mammoth rain towers, brought in case of sunshine and to fill in any naturally occurring gaps in the torrent. Two military Huey choppers arched across the rainswept twilight sky, a twinkling Manhattan skyline in the background. They swooped over a production-designed military command center, an ad hoc suburb of sturdy army green tents, as several cameras in various positions rolled, assisted by assorted giant cranes, including two condor cranes that rose beyond sixty feet into the air; a scissor lift that raised the camera forty feet high; circling searchlights and powerful mini-musco lights that blazed like beacons in the approaching night sky.

"It was a little crazy," admits First Assistant Director Kim Winther, who has known Emmerich and Devlin for seven years. A veteran of several of their films, including *Independence Day* and *StarGate*, Winther thought he'd seen

"The situation on day one of shooting was where we had six or seven cameras shooting helicopters flying over the command center and later that day we had four cameras shooting the scene simultaneously to get a sunset shot. That's a Roland trademark to do these things. On *Independence Day*, we only did that once. On *Godzilla*, we did that at least three times, so I can imagine whatever his next film is, he'll want to do it four, five or six times, and he'll want to shoot it in some country where no one speaks English."

When the company moved into Manhattan, its number only increased. Indeed, almost every sequence filmed in and around New York required several immense lighting rigs, assorted cranes that skimmed the sky, a plethora of cameras, positioned at all altitudes, and hundreds of extras. Even a stunt accomplished that day, choreographed by R. A. Rondell, was literally over-the-top: A crane hoisted a truck cab thirty-five feet in the air, stuntman-cum-truck driver inside, to simulate Godzilla's jaws lifting

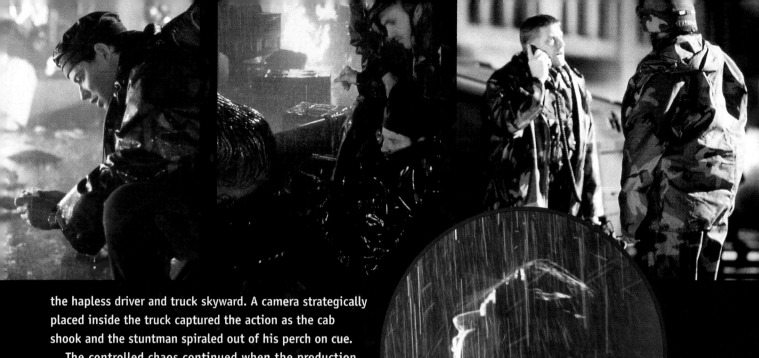

the hapless driver and truck skyward. A camera strategically placed inside the truck captured the action as the cab shook and the stuntman spiraled out of his perch on cue.

The controlled chaos continued when the production moved to Madison Square Park, near the famed Flatiron Building. While the locations department and the producers conscientiously attempted to choose shooting locales that were less residential, there was no getting around it: *Godzilla* was big. One *New York Times* reporter warned the city to expect "two 'huge' lighting rigs, four to five battle tanks, fifty to sixty uniformed soldiers, two big wind generators, one fog machine, and one camera crane." Well, he was close, if one rounds *way* up. Specifically, the following *Godzilla*-created horde invaded Manhattan: an army of 130 soldiers, approximately 200 movie personnel, thirty military vehicles, thirteen cars, four tanks, and a surfeit of movie equipment, from assorted Condor cranes and scissor lifts, multiple cameras and generators, miles of cable and arrays of lights, including five searchlights, three xenons and two mini-muscos. And that's just the stuff that was actually *on* set, without considering the considerable package waiting inside the support trucks in case of an emergency situation.

This immense production bivouacked around Madison Square Park, commandeering several adjacent blocks in the Flatiron District. Lining these narrow streets were trucks bearing lights, gels, c-stands, blacks, props, and cameras; flatbeds securing the giant cranes and trailers, housing the hair and makeup brigade, costumes, actors, producers, and the director. Despite some grumbling, most New Yorkers enjoyed the spectacle. (Although the occasional bystander confused Godzilla with another sometime New York tourist, one oversized primate, asking: "Will Godzilla be on the Empire State Building?") Indeed, a party atmosphere prevailed. While shooting scenes near the famed Flatiron Building, literally hundreds of people filled the adjacent Madison Square Park, warned by an assistant director in advance of the movie-made deluge that drenched the entire square.

■ OPPOSITE PAGE FAR LEFT: *Nose shot of Flatiron Building with three dump trucks dumping fish.*

■ OPPOSITE PAGE CENTER: *Broderick facing crew and fish pile.*

■ BELOW FROM LEFT TO RIGHT: *Storyboard sequence of the Flatiron Building sequence.*

■ INSET: *Nick looks up as Godzilla suddenly appears.*

■ ABOVE FROM LEFT TO RIGHT: *(a) Nick removing a manhole cover. (b) Truck dumping fish into pile. (c) Nick picking up blood samples. (d) Nick being helped from under a fallen statue. (e) Reporting news of the disastrous encounter with Godzilla.*

One night, they watched in astonishment as several bright yellow dump trucks pulled up to dump a load of fish into the center of the street, while the army manned its tanks and Jeeps, weapons raised in anticipation of a giant lizard. The big guy, of course, never appeared, much to the chagrin of several crowd members, not to mention the local media.

Cinematographer Ueli Steiger's frequent and artful use of the Technocrane, a special crane with a telescoping arm and a camera that swivels 360 degrees, provided an amazing display of the Flatiron Building; the shot began tight on Matthew Broderick and, in a single, serpentine motion, became a wide reveal of the set. Like the rest of the crew, Steiger and his department worked within preordained parameters to set up their incredible equipment with as little urban disturbance as possible.

The city only allowed the production, which shot mostly at night, to clear the streets for filming after eight P.M. All the cameras, lights, trucks, related gear and equipment,

personnel, and assorted hordes of extras playing the military or fleeing crowds, had to evaporate from Manhattan thoroughfares by six A.M. A standard film day lasts roughly twelve hours; the city-imposed two-hour deficit, coupled with the short nights typical of spring in New York, could have been terrible setbacks had Emmerich and team not been so organized and efficient.

"We had lots of different, big locations, especially in New York. Essentially, we ended up shooting the wide shots in New York and cheating the tighter ones in Los Angeles," explains Steiger. "Every shot involved a lot of specialized people. Cranes were always involved, and whenever we moved or turned around, we always had big, heavy equipment to move as well. There was always a lot of debris and gravel in the street (the result of Godzilla's enormity and occasional souvenirs of his trip through Manhattan) and the art department always had to rearrange it, depending on the angle we were shooting. That made it incredibly complicated and we had to be very clear about what we were shooting."

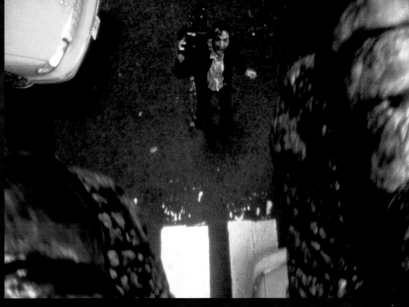

"We had to pre-rig and pre-dress the street, which was difficult because we didn't have much time as we could only shut the street down for so long. Because we shot on major streets in New York, like Madison Avenue, it meant that everything had to be really planned. For us, lighting-wise, that was a really big deal because at night, we saw a lot of the set in the shot. Roland likes to work so that the scene isn't intercut much, so you have to block it in a way where you get a close-up where you

---

■ FAR LEFT FROM TOP TO BOTTOM: *(a) Emmerich setting up daylight street scene. (b) A cop sees Godzilla. (c) Green screens in place for a scene about to be shot. (d) Crowd of umbrellas; crane in background. (e) Police car foreground; businessman running. (f) People running toward police barrier. (g) Emmerich and Bill May on the New York street set.*

■ INSET: *Cabbie looking up in shock.*

■ OPPOSITE PAGE TOP: *Crowd control on street scene.*

■ OPPOSITE PAGE BOTTOM: *People running away while looking back.*

■ RIGHT TOP: *Godzilla's feet leave massive destruction wherever they step.*

■ RIGHT MIDDLE: *Animal gets the shot of a lifetime.*

■ RIGHT BOTTOM: *Side view of Godzilla's foot crunching cars in the street.*

need it and the camera moves to reveal a wider angle. As a matter of principle, we tried to move the camera in each shot to keep a constant flow going, but it meant the entire set, which in this case was several blocks in New York, was in the shot. We had to be incredibly organized, like a military operation, in order to pre-rig in such a short time and to drop all our different generators and cabling in."

"Every movie has another set of problems," Emmerich says philosophically. "A lot of the movie takes place in New York and the creature itself, even if it isn't actually there, is so big that we had to light many more buildings and city blocks than we did in *Independence Day*. A lot of the things we hoped to do in New York we couldn't do there; we had to create total chaos and we could only do it for a short period of time."

*Godzilla* powered through a month of Manhattan filming, moving from Madison Square Park to Wall Street, to Central Park and Forty-fourth and Madison. A scene on Wall Street where Godzilla's "approach" incites hysteria and havoc featured five hundred fleeing day-players and a phalanx of hydraulically rigged cars that "jumped" in response to Godzilla's powerful footsteps. A giant Akela crane (which took four hours to set up) rose seventy-two feet into the air, to provide Godzilla's

INSET UPPER LEFT: *Speech scene showing reflective screen.*

LEFT CENTER: *Special Effects Foreman Emmet Kane positions a 50,000 pound metal plate above a cab, that is soon to be crushed.*

LEFT BOTTOM: *Setup for Animal/Foot sequence.*

RIGHT: *The crowd runs as Godzilla approaches.*

hunched point-of-view of the mayhem resulting from his visit to the world-famous financial district.

Of course, at least two 170-foot-tall rain cranes perpetually soaked the cast and crew, even when Nature complied by providing her own sprinkles. Occasionally, the constant moisture caused the equipment to rebel. Emmerich's experience, coupled with the other equipment available to him, allowed him to compensate for jammed and water-logged gear. On one occasion, Emmerich turned a potential disaster into a serendipity. A small but effective funnel cloud blew across the outdoor set near the Hudson River one afternoon, just before production began, scattering crew

A LOT OF THINGS WE HOPED TO DO IN NEW YORK WE COULDN'T DO THERE; WE HAD TO CREATE TOTAL CHAOS.

members and equipment, sometimes together; the gust sent a light and the electrician hanging on to it skittering down the street. ("Godzilla wasn't on set but it felt like he was," Bill Fay quipped.) The tempest raced across the river toward Manhattan. Emmerich and his camera crew filmed the dramatic, overcast skyline. Assistant cameraman Joe Sanchez, relying on a hunch, kept the cameras rolling, even after the storm had disappeared. His patience paid off: a violent stab of lightning hit one of the Twin Towers of the World Trade Center, *Frankenstein*-style, and appears in the movie.

One of the film's most ambitious shots took place in Central Park. Essentially, the production took over the entire park one stormy night, to film a scene in

ANOTHER DAY - ANOTHER TANK DESIGN .
IDEA FOR TANK WITH HOWITZER CANNON
GODZILLA - 12-19-96 - PATRICK TATOPOULOS

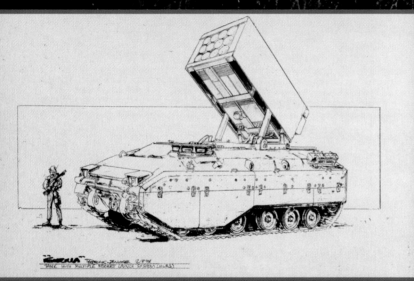

GODZILLA - PATRICK TATOPOULOS 2/4/96
TANK WITH MULTIPLE ROCKET LAUNCH SYSTEM (OURS)

IDEA FOR TROOP TRANSPORT TOP MODULE (T.T.T.M.)
GODZILLA 12/10/96 PATRICK TATOPOULOS

which Sergeant O'Neal and his troops stalk Godzilla, baiting him with a giant fish pile and firing on him as he approaches. Although the city accommodated the production and allowed a battalion of movie personnel, not to mention tanks and other military vehicles, as well as the requisite weaponry to roll into the park, it balked at a huge mountain of fish. So, Godzilla and his cuisine would be composited into the shot in post-production.

"We were pretty pumped for that shot," First Assistant Director Kim Winther recalls. "It was similar to a rooftop shot we had done on *Independence Day*, where we had four or five cameras shooting simultaneously from different angles and different vignettes happening at various camera positions. We coordinated it from one position, where Roland was, so we had microwave feeds from each camera so he could direct all the action. It required a great deal of planning and timing; we had to place everybody on different rooftops, set up spotlights, coordinate gunfire. When everything was ready, we had to tell everyone to roll camera and it took three or four minutes to make sure on the monitors that everyone was rolling. Then we filmed all these things happening at once. It was exciting. Actually, it was about six or seven hours of preparing for about thirty minutes of filming, but after you've completed a shot like this, the buzz you get at the end of the day, which in this case was dawn, is great."

Winther mobilized these complicated camera setups and the positioning of "the military" in the vast set commonly known as Central Park with the help of a cadre of production assistants and the Second Assistant Director, Lars Winther. Lars also happens to be Kim's younger brother and much of the logistical organization was his responsibility.

"What happened was we had five cameras. One was on the Bergdorf Building looking down at the park. That was Godzilla's POV. We had another camera at Sixty-eighth and Fifth Avenue, which is what we call the spotters rooftop. We had about eight extras and one actor up there and they all had their guns ready, as they watched for Godzilla. That was a

Steadicam shot; it panned down Fifth Avenue, looking for Godzilla. Then, in the Sheep Meadow, we had a Vista Vision camera (for plate shots), looking toward Grand Army Plaza. We saw some tanks and vehicles there, with about twenty military extras, all ready for Godzilla. In the foreground of the Sheep Meadow would be a CGI fish pile and CGI helicopters because the city wouldn't let us put anything like that in the park. At the entrance to the Park, near the Plaza Hotel, we had about fifty extras and Doug Savant, as Sergeant O'Neal, all waiting for Godzilla."

Of course, Godzilla eventually arrived, but only later via the computer. On location, as usual, everyone had to imagine his colossal presence. Only in this case, the troops also had to fire at him. Gunfire was a tricky issue in Manhattan; initially, the production tested a fusillade in the Flatiron District, which proved to be quite deafening. By the time the production moved to Central Park, the effects department had muffled the guns considerably. Still, the troops had to shoot at *something*.

"One of the landmarks we had to shoot at was the Plaza Hotel, which was right about where Godzilla was supposed to be," Savant recalls. "It was five in the morning, the sun was coming up, the morning commute was beginning, and we were fighting Godzilla. We had these beams of light plastered on the Plaza Hotel and guys were shooting off hundreds of rounds while the AD, trying to give us motivation, shouted over the bullhorn, 'We hate the Plaza.' That was the highlight of shooting in Central Park for me."

The company traveled to Los Angeles after completing photography in New York. In Los Angeles, the production divided its time between downtown locations, Long Beach, the Sony lot and a stint at Falls Lake, at Universal Studios. Several downtown locations were familiar to alumni of *Independence Day*. The Second and Third Street tunnels doubled as Gotham's Lincoln Tunnel and the Park Avenue viaduct in *Godzilla*, but the opposite ends of the respective locales appeared in *Independence Day* as well. Although the films shared locations, that's where comparison ended, according to Location Manager Ken Fix, who served in the same capacity on *Independence Day*.

"The amount of equipment and vehicles we had to move every night was staggering, much harder than what we had to do on *Independence Day*. The logistics were frightening, but somehow, we made it work, with the help of the city and the EIDC (Entertainment Industry Development Corporation)."

One of the most impressive shots took place in downtown Los Angeles at Seventh Street and Santa Fe Avenue, which served as the Brooklyn Bridge. A carefully orchestrated traffic jam of epic proportions, featuring 450 cars and

■ ABOVE INSET: *Peter Winther.*

■ LEFT FROM TOP TO BOTTOM: *(a) Roland Emmerich on the beach in Hawaii, directing the setup for a scene. (b) Dean Devlin giving an interview on the street in New York. In the background is a giant crane used in the shoot. (c) Emmerich is dressed as military crew in a helicopter as they prepare to shoot a scene from a moving platform. (d) Hank Azaria and Dean Devlin in an off-screen moment. (e) Ute Emmerich (f) Dean Devlin enjoys a lighter moment. (g) Dean Devlin and Matthew Broderick between takes on the set.*

■ BELOW: *Emmerich stands in front of the model for Godzilla's toes showing how the scene with Animal (Hank Azaria) will be framed and shot.*

assorted trucks and buses, lined the incline leading up to the bridge, all behind a barricade of military vehicles that cleared an area at the top of the bridge. There, the "hero" vehicle was to speed up a slight ramp and career into the pavement, fishtailing to a stop in front of the military. The first take really tested the stunt driver's reflexes; as the car hit the pavement, the electricity died, causing the lights to shut off and the power steering to freeze. The car skidded and screeched to a halt, but, in this case, with a little more authenticity than originally intended.

Although this scene and many others took place in the city at night in the rain, the set featured many surprisingly colorful accents. These hues came mostly from the lighting, whether that was the glow of traffic lights and streetlights or the luminance of movie lights and gels.

"Roland, Jim Grce (the gaffer) and I talked a lot about how a city looks at night and how to light that. We noticed that even though it is dark and the city is asleep, it isn't colorless. We decided to go with a really warm look for the streets, as if it were lit from the

◼ LEFT FROM TOP TO BOTTOM: *(a) A look from behind reflective screens at the staging for the shot of the dropping truck at the Fulton Fish Market. (b) Camera crew on a moving cart adjust the focus on a shot. (c) Script supervisor Kim Berner gives Hank Azaria a Godzilla eyeline. (d) Another view of a camera crew at work. (e) Over the shoulders of a camera crew as they capture an action sequence. (f) A moment during the final cab chase scene which shows a camera truck moving beside the cab. (g) Green screens covering equipment as a New York street scene is about to be shot.*

◼ RIGHT FROM TOP TO BOTTOM: *(a) A closer look at the camera truck and crew. (b) Cinematographer Ueli Steiger looks over to receive directions about where he will be aiming and moving the camera. (c) Emmerich sits with the camera crew to watch what's in the frame as a scene unfolds.*

architecture of the city, from street lights and interior buildings," Cinematographer Ueli Steiger says. "We also always had to backlight the rain. We lit that separately, in a half-blue, to give a mixture of color to the sets. That color scheme went through the whole film, this mixture of warm and cold light."

Some of the lights, like many of the shots, were kinetic and the occasional xenon light and an electrician became a practical part of the scene.

"One of the key things we used were xenons, hard beams of light that look like searchlights. A few times, we put searchlights in our Humvees, which were the key military vehicles chasing Godzilla during a big scene in the Flatiron section. We actually put a couple of our electricians in costume, stuck them in Humvees and got battery packs for the xenons. We'd always find a reason to use them or some type of light that moved through frame. Most of the film was lit by a moving light. We'd have electricians shaking or whirling lights. We also used a

■ TOP FROM LEFT TO RIGHT: *(a) Camera crew films the weaponry in Phillipe Roache's hideout. (b) Setup in the Fulton Fish Market. Note camera under an umbrella covering. (c) Camera track showing in foreground in the setup for the Fulton Fish Market scene. (d) Close-up of stunt actor falling. (e) A camera crew surrounds a helicopter. (f) Actors running into the Fulton Fish Market setup.*

■ INSET: *Dean Devlin wearing a cap from his television series,* The Visitor.

■ LEFT CENTER: *Big net with debris being raised by a crane in preparation for the Fulton Fish Market scene.*

■ LEFT BOTTOM: *Matthew Broderick watches as worms are prepared for the Chernobyl sequence. Roland Emmerich also looks on.*

■ RIGHT FROM TOP TO BOTTOM: *(a) Matthew Broderick tries to wave off the helicopter landing near Chernobyl. (b) Broderick plays scientist Dr. Nick Tatopoulos researching irradiated worms near Chernobyl.*

lot of interactive lighting, fire lights that pulsed to simulate explosions or sometimes they just added to the ambiance or tone of the scene. We also used a lot of lightning flashes in the rain, so that it could be very dark and the lightning would give a hint as to where we were."

Because Godzilla's size predicated that a vast area of the city would be seen in most shots, Grce and his team not only had to light the immediate set but several blocks beyond it. For a shot that took place in downtown Los Angeles' Pershing Square, which doubled for the exterior Madison Square Garden, " we also had to light two or three blocks down from the set in an easterly direction, as well as a block in the southerly direction and two and a half blocks north, so that when we were in the inner, main section, the surrounding areas wouldn't be completely dark. You can't just light one main pocket where the live action is and have everything else go black, it would look very weird," Grce says.

To accomplish this, Grce's team used a variety of lights, from dinos, (occasionally controlled by a computerized dimmer board), to xenons to mini-muscos. These lumens not only brightened up the night, they provided interactive lighting to simulate the explosion of Madison Square Garden, which meets a fiery end, like the White House in *Independence Day*. Of course, the production couldn't actually blow up Pershing Square. That's where Grce's magical lighting came into play.

"We had had six dino lights mounted. Each dino light has twenty-four 1000 watt pars in it, so that's 130 something or another. And we had this very warm gel on it and what we'd done was to put it all on a dimmer board, so that on cue, when Madison Square Garden gets bombed, we could bring up this whole bright light and just flood the inner section with something that mimics an explosion and then burning firelight. So, it's on cue and we just kept this going throughout the scene so that when we cut to the model which explodes and this wall of fire comes up, we cut back into the live action here and it all sort of blends together," Grce explains.

To ready this array of light for shooting required an around-the-clock crew.

"What happened was we'd shoot a street at night and then the rigging team would come in and strike the equipment from that street in the morning and then move it to our next one. They'd build it all up at that location, then we'd come in at six o'clock in the evening and shoot that street. We basically had a twenty-four-hour crew," Grce explains.

Another crew worked on a parallel schedule: the second unit film team, overseen by Co-producer Peter Winther. He'd begun this work in New York. His compact unit scoured the city at all hours, filming assorted shots with several camera rigs, varying the film frame speeds, to give Emmerich choices when he adds the required special effects to complete the sequences later. Such shots included swooping motion control moves, to simulate helicopters zooming through the urban canyons; huge, vaulting pans, from earth to sky and back, representing Godzilla's massive footsteps as he marches through Gotham, and static plate shots, revealing vistas of the city and its world-famous monuments.

In Los Angeles, when the first unit team shot on downtown locations, Winther's second unit was invariably nearby, filming the scenes that would augment the main photography.

"We have large scale chaos scenes where people are running away from Godzilla. Because of the time frame of short nights in New York and the time when we could actually get on the streets and set up the equipment, put

■ LEFT: *A sequence of story-boards shows the descent into a ruined subway station, the discovery of Godzilla's tunnel and the progress toward a near encounter with Godzilla.*

■ TOP: *Nick and Phillipe Roache lead an exploration through the tunnels.*

■ ABOVE: *Pre-production painting showing the planned scene down to the rubble and the flashlight beams.*

■ RIGHT FROM TOP TO BOTTOM: *(a) Another scene of the team in the tunnels. (b) Everybody looks up. (c) Close-up on Roache in the tunnels. (d) Nick's face lit by the flashlight beam.*

up the rain rigs, set up the extras, Roland was only really able to get the action with the principals. He wasn't able to establish a lot of the environment surrounding that action. He was never able to personify the other people in the city reacting to Godzilla and you need to show that the entire city is being affected. The second unit shot all those reactions, from the military and the chaos, to establish that environment so that the personal stories of the heroes have some context," Winther notes.

Winther's second unit also shot on stages at Sony, using the footage he and Engel filmed from the perch of their New York helicopter in a time-honored technique known as rear-screen projection.

"We used a lot of rear-screen projection instead of green screen on *Godzilla*. Rear projection is where you take a background plate you've shot beforehand, for example, the plate we shot of New York City from the helicopter. You take that film and project it from behind the screen but it's reversed, so when you put it on the screen it runs forward. We put an Apache cockpit in the foreground and you can see the city going by in the rear projection. The advantage is that it's all an in-camera shot. You can shoot smoke going by, you can shake the camera, whatever you want. It saves money because with green screen, it becomes a composite (where the background is added in later by computer) and smoke has to be rotoscoped (added or drawn by hand on a frame-by-frame basis) in every time. It's an old technique, but, if it ain't broke . . ."

Of course, the Apache pilots chased Godzilla and whenever their gargantuan target appeared in the shot, green screen had to be employed.

"If Godzilla was in frame, then we had to go to green screen because to do rear projection with the cockpit and then add Godzilla to that would be very difficult and expensive," Winther explains. "So, we would shoot the entire sequence rear projection and then setup a green screen and project green through the rear projection

soundstage a full-scale embodiment of the creature's giant
jaws rested atop a gimbal. Inside the terrible maw perched
a full-scale cab, in which the four principal actors sat. As
the gimbal rocked the ferocious gullet, the actors
attempted to "drive" away from a Jonah-like end.

One of the most challenging sets was the remains of the
Twenty-third Street subway station, a tattered platform that
had crumbled into the sewers below, due to Godzilla's
unique march through Manhattan. Production Designer
Oliver Scholl built the subway platform and sewer tunnel on
Stage 29 at Sony, a space with eighty-foot-tall ceilings.
Scholl's team took advantage of the stage's height.

"We tried to create scale with that set, to build
something that really transferred Godzilla's scale into
reality. So, we built the platform thirty-eight feet off the
ground and the tunnel itself was fifty feet high. It was
about dwarfing people, because Godzilla created this vast
trench, so if the subway station set dwarfs the actors, who
are standing on top of the platform looking down at this
giant hole, it translates into Godzilla's size."

Similar to a sequence in *Independence Day* that revealed
a captive spaceship for the first time, Scholl and his team
designed the subway set for one main shot.

"The subway set was similar to the hangar set where
the attacker (spaceship) was housed in *Independence
Day*, in that they were both laid out for one main shot. In
the subway, the shot was from the end of the tunnel
toward the really high platform of the subway station. If

----

■ LEFT: *The new Godzilla can move underground, a fact that required
the construction of several tunnel pieces that had to match the tunnel
for the live action–shoot exactly. Modelmaker Tony Ciccarelli adds
final touches to the twenty-fourth scale model.*

■ BELOW: *A storyboard sequence showing Nick running to an elevator
pursued by Baby Godzillas, pounding the elevator button, the doors
closing on the head of a Baby Godzilla and then kicking the Baby to
get its head out of the doorway.*

it wasn't for that shot, we could have built the platform a bit lower, but to arrange it so that the shot came within the center of the circle of the tunnel floor, from that perspective, we needed to elevate the platform, even though Roland really hates heights. It worked out nicely, actually. With the spotlights going up and down, showing glimpses of the void, it gave the sense of the size and impact of the creature."

This massive set revealed not only the shattered subway station but the labyrinth of the sewer below. This wily creature not only stomps through Manhattan, he burrows beneath it. "In our research, we discovered that certain types of lizards are able to burrow, so we decided to give Godzilla that talent," Devlin says. It was Scholl's job, however, to depict the devastating consequences of that ability. To do so, he also did some research, into the murky past of New York City.

It was tricky because we were trying to portray a phenomenon that luckily hasn't happened, that something digs out an eighty-foot or even bigger tunnel underneath New York, through all the subway and sewer lines and conducting and electrical systems and everything. So, even though it seems straightforward, because it is supposed to be real, it was actually not straightforward at all. What we did is we looked at a lot of photo research on tunnel-working utility lines in New York and utility renovations in New York where you see really huge underground tunnels being dug out. But they are still small in scale compared to ours. The interesting thing about New York is that the city really continues hundreds of feet beneath the city. You're going into, for example, buildings that maybe have underground parking lots and then you have electrical phone lines, old sewer systems, old drainage systems, old phone lines

and old subway shafts. It goes further and further down so the newest sewer systems go very far down underneath New York. Also, there are foundations of the buildings that are deeper than the parking lot structures, for example. So, you get pretty interesting cross sections through the city. Of course, portraying that in a set of fifty or eighty feet high is not really possible, but you can bring in elements that kind of give you the idea of what happened. So, we had bricks from old sewers down there, we had concrete from newer sewers, we had electrical power lines lying around, we added fallen turnstiles from the subway system there, we stuck vending machines in the set and cars from the parking lot that fell all the way down. The idea was to convey a sense of all those layers characterized by the rubble that was there."

Scholl's vision became a practical set via Construction Coordinator Gary Krakoff. The subway set, he says, took a month to build and prior to construction of all the sets, he began to hoard lumber in anticipation of the mammoth job ahead.

"The first week, while they were laying out the set, we researched every material available, everything we could get in quantity, because of the huge size of the set. We ended up getting samples of different kinds of wall textures, found out that Styrofoam worked the best with the type of design it required, lots of sculpting and all that (for the rocks and debris in the subway/sewer). We ordered the whole amount of lumber way in advance— that's why this lot was full of trucks—only to be assured that we could get it because sometimes there is a run on lumber, with so many people building in town," Krakoff explains.

Krakoff adds that the altitude and configuration of the set presented a construction challenge, but his overall concern was to build a set that was structurally safe.

"There was a heavy emphasis on structural safety because one side of our set was eighty feet tall, so that had to be incorporated prior to us starting to

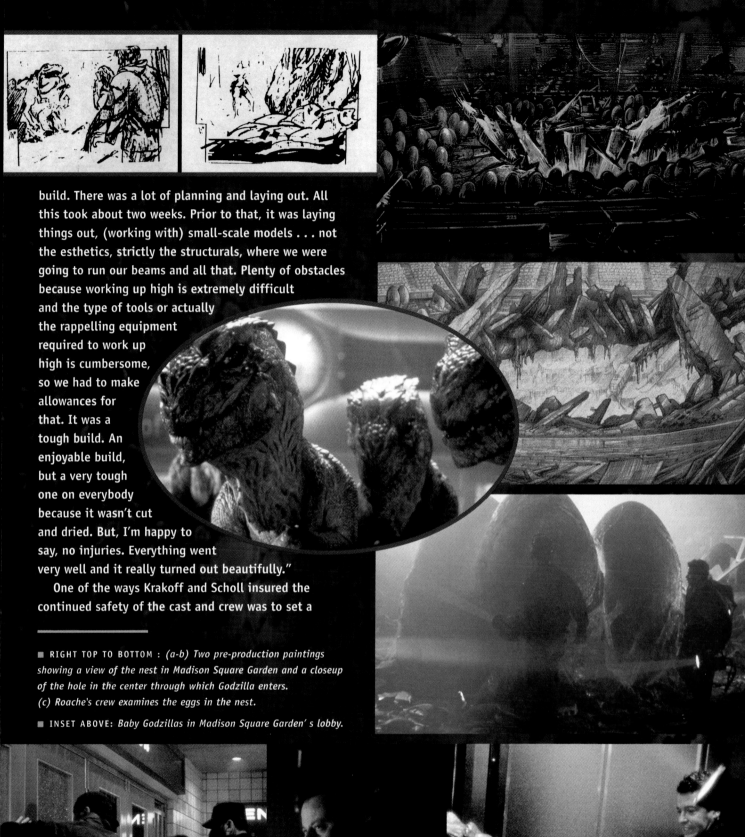

build. There was a lot of planning and laying out. All this took about two weeks. Prior to that, it was laying things out, (working with) small-scale models . . . not the esthetics, strictly the structurals, where we were going to run our beams and all that. Plenty of obstacles because working up high is extremely difficult and the type of tools or actually the rappelling equipment required to work up high is cumbersome, so we had to make allowances for that. It was a tough build. An enjoyable build, but a very tough one on everybody because it wasn't cut and dried. But, I'm happy to say, no injuries. Everything went very well and it really turned out beautifully."

One of the ways Krakoff and Scholl insured the continued safety of the cast and crew was to set a

■ RIGHT TOP TO BOTTOM : *(a-b) Two pre-production paintings showing a view of the nest in Madison Square Garden and a closeup of the hole in the center through which Godzilla enters. (c) Roache's crew examines the eggs in the nest.*

■ INSET ABOVE: *Baby Godzillas in Madison Square Garden's lobby.*

limit, in terms of the amount of personnel allowed on the platform that overlooked the "sewer" below.

"We put a limit as to how many people could be up there (thirty people) . . , that deck will hold 200 people, but safely, thirty. Mainly it wasn't the weight but the configuration of the open edges. If you got too many people up there, one person could easily become disoriented. So, I personally put a limit on it and then asked the assistant directors if they would honor it. They almost always go by what we tell them when it involves safety. It was dark and smoky up there when we were shooting, with jagged edges and there were parts (of the platform) that were Styrofoam up there, on the very edge. It looked like concrete, but after a certain point, it was just Styrofoam and someone could easily have fallen through it."

The Styrofoam-cum-concrete was sturdier than the average foam packing. It was specially treated stuff, able to withstand the rigors of shooting.

"All the interior was sculpted, all the rock formations . . . our plasterers went over that with a plaster coating so that people could climb on the rocks, to add to their strength. And then we had the secondary plasterers come down and define the rocks, they put plaster on them to redefine the rocks, to give them a little definition, to redefine and sculpt them. So, it was sort of a three-stage operation, with the plastering, sculpting and painting," Krakoff says. Additionally, Krakoff's team "beefed up the superstructure," which was so strong it was able to

sustain several key pieces of set decoration embedded in the ruins, including a fallen soda vending machine and a real subway car.

As impressive as the subway set was the interior of Madison Square Garden, which actually spread over three stages. Stage 15 housed the hallway and broadcast booth and Stage 29 became the interior entrance, but Stage 30 served as the Garden proper. Or, at least what was left of it, after Godzilla moved in. It seems that Godzilla, like the Knicks, found Madison Square Garden to be the perfect home. The beloved stadium became an incubator, where Godzilla's many offspring hatched from sticky, oversized eggs.

The set was a tricky construct, since part of it had to affect various degrees of Godzilla-induced destruction, yet it also had to sustain a cast and crew and the tools of moviemaking, from cameras to lights. Plus, Scholl had to work around the sound—stage's peculiar architectural "enhancements": The hoary Sony soundstage featured a tank, from the days when Esther Williams swam her way to stardom. Designing the MSG set, as the crew referred to it, was an exercise in trial and error, as Scholl recalls, and ultimately, he just split the difference between the pristine and demolished portions of the set.

"Madison Square Garden had a long history of approaches that led to the

design we ended up building. In the beginning, we just wanted to have a development between the sets (on Stages 15, 29, and 30) and the general look of the situation: what happens when Godzilla breaks through the walls and lays his eggs, so it was a pretty simple premise. But, it leads to 20,000 variations. So, you go through a few variations: What does it look like with the eggs lying in there, how does the hallway look? What it came down to, I wanted to have a way of discerning the two sides of the set because of the geometry of the stage, having the tank on one side and at one point we wanted to have the people in the broadcast booth actually on that set and rope down, although we got around that by building a separate broadcast booth set. Anyway, I needed the height, so I wanted to find a way to use the height of that tank, though I couldn't use it if we ramped the whole thing over to build the normal seating areas. So, I thought with the gigantic weight and mass of the creature, it probably would have collapsed on one side, so that's how we came up with the good side and bad side idea."

Erecting this version of Madison Square Garden was as complicated as designing it. As Gary Krakoff recalls, the smashed side of the Garden was actually more difficult to build than the pristine portion.

"The auditorium was also challenging because that set also rose almost eighty feet. It started out on the floor, with a good side and a bad side.

One side started with the stairs leading to the seats, with the superstructure down below. In building the superstructure, we had to allow for other departments to put their equipment there, including the creature shop. So, there we had to plan really a series of structural supports to make sure that what was up above did not come down on them.

"There were actually two sets in one. The first side was the steps and seating areas, with various tunnels. The other side was actually a lot more difficult because the other side is the destroyed side. Since we needed to see through it, we couldn't build it out of lumber. We had to build it out of steel support so we could have larger spans without support, to be able to look through a wall of the destroyed side and see the tunnels or where the vendor areas would be, whatever. So, that whole side of the structure was made of steel. The flooring was wood, but it was basically a steel structure, so that was actually one of the tougher

large shards as if the tunnel floor and a slab of concrete was ripped out. All that was sculpted. That also took about twelve weeks."

A recurring theme in both the sewer and Madison Square Garden sets was fish. Not only did Godzilla feed on the slimy delicacy, but so did his young. Consequently, a trail of fish from the sewer led to mounds of it in Madison Square Garden, sustenance the caring beast brought for his young. Some of the fish were radio-controlled props, designed to flop and twitch on cue. Others were more fetid and less talented. Still more only existed in the computer.

"Fish was the theme of the movie. Fish was the bait and naturally because the animal is big, it's like if you have a very big dog, the portions get bigger, and Godzilla eats tons and tons of fish. At the Flatiron, we needed to have a truckload of fish, which we dumped in the street several times, so we had to build them out of rubber because real fish would never hold like that. And then later we had to build the whole pile in CG, in the computer, in 3-D. And then in Madison Square Garden, fish had to be everywhere, actually there were fish everywhere but they were kind of these soft things. You were walking funny all day, because they were kind of sticky in a way. They'd get sticky and dirty. We had foreground fish and background fish, we had real hero fish, we had flopping hero fish. Doug Harlocker, the prop man, had fish for every occasion," Emmerich recalls.

In contrast to the vast, fish-filled Madison Square Garden and subway set, Oliver Scholl also had to create smaller settings, from the utilitarian military command center, all corrugated metal and army green, to the cozy interior of Lucy and Animal's apartment. In contrast to the darkness and danger outside, Scholl wanted this to be a welcoming, warm haven. "The idea was that the interior apartment would be homey, juxtaposed against the outside, where the monster is, which becomes cold and eerie," Scholl explains.

To convey this "homey" feeling, Scholl used "muted colors—browns, off-greens, and yellows, in a sort of layered effect. It's as if the house went through two or three renovations and some of them were more successful than others. It's definitely a place that has been lived in."

■ LEFT FROM TOP TO BOTTOM: *(a) A store clerk sells Nick a collection of pregnancy test kits. (b) Nick works on the tests. (c) A close-up look at Nick's experiments. (d) Nick tells Audrey his conclusions.*

■ RIGHT: *Audrey and Lucy in the rain.*

■ FAR RIGHT: *Spots of costume color against a drab background.*

■ INSET ABOVE RIGHT: *Lucy shows off her style.*

Scholl worked closely with Emmerich and Costume Designer Joseph Porro to determine the movie's color palette and overall tone.

"Color scheme is a funny thing. Sometimes you have a predetermined color in mind. Sometimes you just select colors, based on a general mood. After going through some color combinations and talking with Roland and Joseph, things filtered into place. We found that we had a seventies touch, from the costumes to the colors to some of the furniture styles," Scholl says.

The concept of using styles from the seventies, Porro adds, was "to give the costumes a hipness. Roland wanted the clothes to be non descript but to have an edge. I guess you could say that my inspiration was old pattern books from the 1960s and 1970s for the women. For the guys, we worked with Diesel and Hugo Boss, so they had some great stuff."

Much of the movie's color, when not emanating from the lighting, comes from Porro's costumes. " I generally used oranges that go into browns, burgundy that became deeper reds and a lot of green. Green is usually a color I avoid, but we used it purposely, to add a grittier feel." Occasionally, Porro utilized a bright pop of color, to stand out against the darkness and perpetual rain.

"In my initial conversations with Roland, I commented that once you put rain on clothing, it gets very, very dark, unless you've got

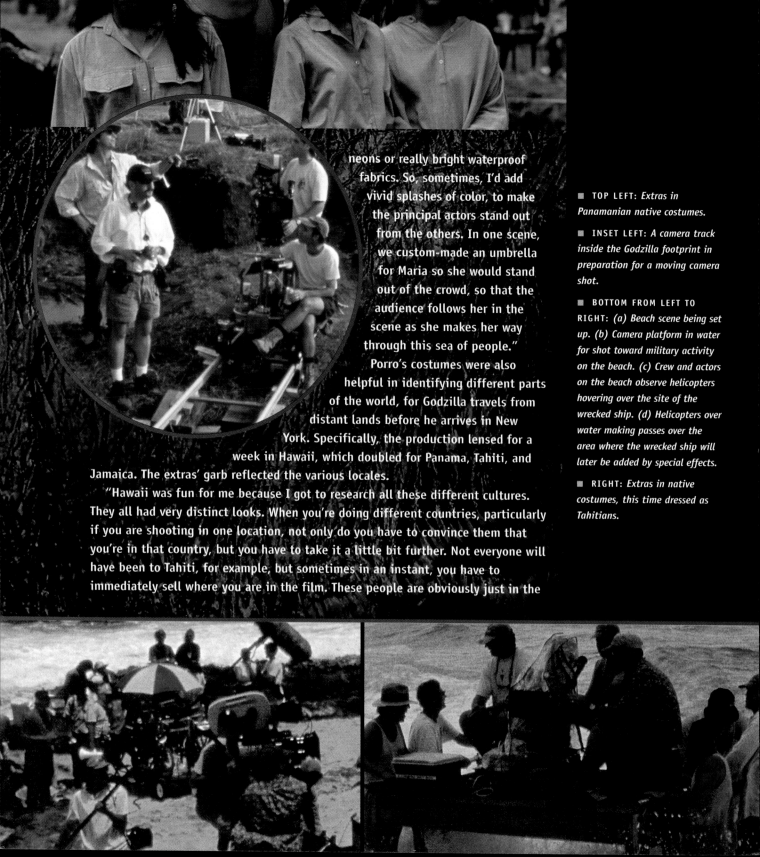

neons or really bright waterproof fabrics. So, sometimes, I'd add vivid splashes of color, to make the principal actors stand out from the others. In one scene, we custom-made an umbrella for Maria so she would stand out of the crowd, so that the audience follows her in the scene as she makes her way through this sea of people."

Porro's costumes were also helpful in identifying different parts of the world, for Godzilla travels from distant lands before he arrives in New York. Specifically, the production lensed for a week in Hawaii, which doubled for Panama, Tahiti, and Jamaica. The extras' garb reflected the various locales.

"Hawaii was fun for me because I got to research all these different cultures. They all had very distinct looks. When you're doing different countries, particularly if you are shooting in one location, not only do you have to convince them that you're in that country, but you have to take it a little bit further. Not everyone will have been to Tahiti, for example, but sometimes in an instant, you have to immediately sell where you are in the film. These people are obviously just in the

■ TOP LEFT: *Extras in Panamanian native costumes.*

■ INSET LEFT: *A camera track inside the Godzilla footprint in preparation for a moving camera shot.*

■ BOTTOM FROM LEFT TO RIGHT: *(a) Beach scene being set up. (b) Camera platform in water for shot toward military activity on the beach. (c) Crew and actors on the beach observe helicopters hovering over the site of the wrecked ship. (d) Helicopters over water making passes over the area where the wrecked ship will later be added by special effects.*

■ RIGHT: *Extras in native costumes, this time dressed as Tahitians.*

background, but as they walk by, they have to tell the audience that it is in Tahiti or Panama or Jamaica. So, what I did was give the audience more than what they might see in reality, so they would know where it was."

To do this, Porro meticulously researched native attire and used color as a tool.

"For our Panamanian Indians, we found a woman who collects native clothing from a particular tribe and put some of the extras in it. The Panamanians tend to wear much more washed-out colors and a distinctive kind of shirt. They also wear a lot of hats. In Jamaica, the women will wear straw hats, but the men tend to wear caps. Jamaicans favor bright reds, oranges and yellows. In Tahiti, they go for these distinct floral patterns."

All of these countries actually were separate locations on the north shore of Oahu. The entire week *Godzilla* shot there was devoid of trade winds and abnormally hot. Shooting began promptly at six a.m., to maximize as many shooting hours as possible, since the sun set by seven p.m. The first location was in a verdant valley at Kualoa Ranch, where, prior to filming, the entire company was blessed in a traditional Hawaiian ceremony. Although the filmmakers happened upon the ranch by accident, on a location scout, the glen and surrounding hills are familiar film spots, as became evident as the cast and crew arrived. At the entrance sits a giant *Jurassic Park* sign. *Godzilla* added its own mark to the ranch, quite literally. An advance team labored for a month to stamp the monster's huge footprint into the soft grass. Emmerich filmed Godzilla's tracks from above, with the help of an Akela crane and

several helicopter fly-bys. In fact, the director suited up in pilot costume for one of the shots, in case the camera happened to catch him in the chopper.

The company also shot in two historic Oahu locations in one day, beginning at Mark's Pier and ending up at Kualoa State Beach. Mark's Pier, a long, wooden pier made less rickety for the film crew by an advance team, doubled for Panama. A weird, dense fog hung over the production, which arrived at the usual early hour. A large dock at the end provided the base for the filmmakers. Among the Panamanian set dressing sat a talkative parrot and as the camera crew set up the shot, Emmerich taught it to say "Gojira." Opposite the dock sat an old-fashioned, silvery seaplane, bobbing in the water, from which Matthew Broderick emerged. The plane had originally been white, but the art department painted it silver for the shot. Combined with the low clouds and mist, it looked like a scene out of *Casablanca*. (This image was later dispelled when second unit shot it in flight. As it sailed through the sky, the temporary paint began to fly off the fuselage.)

■ TOP LEFT TO RIGHT: *(a) Setting up footprint scene. (b) Nick standing in the giant footprint as he begins to realize just exactly what's going on. (c) Close-up of Nick in the footprint.*

■ LEFT TOP TO BOTTOM: *Four pre-production paintings showing concepts for the footprint discovery scene. (a) The jungle setting near where the footprint is being examined. (b) Another view of the setting for the footprint. (c) Plan for the seaplane arrival scene at the long pier filled with local natives. (d) A view of how the path Godzilla has smashed through the jungle will look.*

■ INSET ABOVE: *Nick on the beach gazing up at the wreck of the ship. Phillipe Roache is visible in the background.*

■ INSET RIGHT: *A shot of a destroyed native shack left behind by Godzilla.*

■ RIGHT: *A shot of some native extras on the porch of a building partially destroyed by Godzilla..*

As the scene progressed, Broderick, escorted by Kevin Dunn's Colonel Hicks, strode down the pier through a gang of reporters and curious Panama locals clambering up the sides of the dock from speed boats, rowboats, and small pontoons. A few of the press were actually real local Hawaii reporters, anxious to cover the Hawaiian portion of *Godzilla*. As the scene was filmed through the lens of a Steadicam, which captured nearly every portion of the pier, there was no other place to put the press than in the shot itself.

By noon, the fog had cleared, just in time for lunch and a company move to Kualoa Beach Park. In the parking lot, the art and construction departments had erected the facade of a hospital. The scene was one in which Jean Reno's Phillipe Roache enters a Tahitian hospital to interrogate the sole survivor of a sunken freighter — a former Japanese floating fish cannery, destroyed by the ravenous Godzilla. The interior interrogation scenes had been filmed in Los Angeles but the exterior demanded something more tropical than the Sony lot. Palm fronds and bougainvillea were brought in to mimic the desired atmosphere, but Steiger's camera crew had to position the shot just right. Otherwise, the distinctive green knoll, Chinaman's Hat, rising from the sea, would betray the decidedly Hawaiian location.

After the hectic week in Hawaii, the production returned to

Los Angeles for more filming. At this point, second unit became first unit. After completing the primary scenes with the actors, Emmerich helmed some key second unit sequences that didn't include the main thespians. These portions of the movie were critical and complicated, so they required the director's attention.

One of the most rigorous shoots on this schedule took place at Falls Lake, at Universal Studios. During the day, this sizable body of water is part of the Universal Studio's tour and indeed, driving to location was like traveling through Hollywood history. En route, the crew passed the Bates Motel, a remnant of the set of *Jurassic Park* and a sign welcoming travelers to Amity. The latter landmark was in keeping with

■ LEFT FROM TOP TO BOTTOM: *(a) A long shot of the seaplane arriving at the dock in Jamaica. (b) A closer view of the dock with the seaplane and milling crowds. (c) A view of small boats filled with reporters as the seaplane is being unloaded onto the dock. (d) A close-up of the seaplane at dockside.*

■ INSET ABOVE: *Vicki Lewis, sitting by the beach, waiting for the call to do a scene as Dr. Elsie Chapman, who helps examine the destroyed ship on the beach.*

■ INSET RIGHT: *Phillipe Roache about to have his first encounter with the U.S. military and with Dr. Nick Tatopoulos.*

■ OPPOSITE PAGE CLOCKWISE FROM UPPER LEFT: *(a) Seaplane at the dock as Nick, accompanied by a military escort, proceeds landward. (b) Helicopters over beach with military scattered around. (c) Roache exits vehicle on his way to interrogate the lone survivor of the Japanese fish factory ship. (d) Setup in process for the beach scene. The ladder is being used to mark the focus point for the ship which will be added later using CG.*

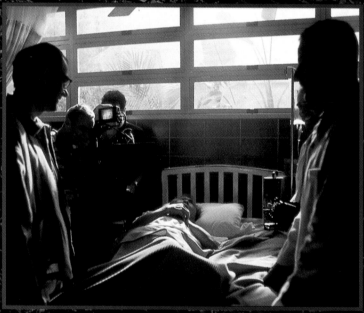

■ TOP: *Scene set in Tahitian hospital with lone survivor.*

■ ABOVE: *Another angle on the scene in the hosiptal room in Tahiti.*

■ OPPOSITE PAGE TOP: *Visual Effects Supervisor Volker Engel (left) and Visual Effects Producer Terry Clotiaux on the Falls Lake set in discussion about the setup of the fishing trawler sequence.*

■ INSET: *Dr. Chapman and Nick viewing information on monitor.*

■ OPPOSITE PAGE BOTTOM: *One of the trawlers in the water at Falls Lake being readied for the dramatic scene where it is pulled under and then bobs to the surface again.*

the Zeitgeist of the scene shot there for *Godzilla*, for it was a blatant homage to *Jaws*. It involved three fishing trawlers, dragged underwater by Godzilla, the way the Great White shark submerged so many barrels in Spielberg's classic horror adventure. While model fishing boats actually sank, Emmerich and company had to shoot a full-size fishing boat plummeting into the dark water, so that actors playing the fishermen could leap off the doomed barge.

Although Falls Lake is large, it was dwarfed by all the movie equipment and trucks parked on its shores, as well as assorted camera gear on vessels in the lake. Of course, ubiquitous twin rain cranes towered overhead, as did as a huge Chapman crane, swooping over the lake to ferry the lights above the set. Several oversized fans waited on the banks, to provide a tempest of wind on cue. New machinery also graced this set, including a wave machine that resembled two huge milk crates with a fulcrum inside to push the water around. An overgrown tow truck, called a Tom John, sat opposite the carefully weathered dinghy, a faded green and white boat that came to life when a row of soft yellow lights inside and some red and green ones on the top suddenly switched on as the sun went down. On Emmerich's command, the rain, wind, and waves began, the Tom John inched backward and the boat, attached via underwater cable to the truck, slid into the depths of the lake, gliding along a pre-installed track, buried in the water. Three strategically placed cameras, plus a Hydroflex camera under water, captured the action and the crew applauded as Emmerich called "cut."

The day prior to this shot, Emmerich had lensed some establishing shots that required the 46,000 pound boat to float. So, they created a buoyant trawler equipped with special flotation devices. In order for the skiff to sink the next evening, the mechanical effects squadron removed the flotation devices and rigged it with small wheels, akin to those on an airplane, so it would slide down the hidden steel ramp. The shot went extremely well but repositioning the boat on the track for another take proved to be as difficult as the shot. It seemed that the fishing boat had fallen off its guiding track and it took several tries and various maneuvers with the tow truck to reposition it. Finally returned to its proper place, Emmerich executed the second shot flawlessly, albeit after "lunch," at about one-thirty A.M.

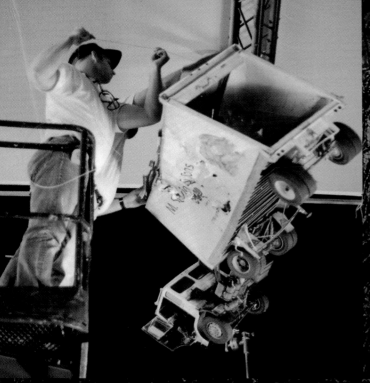

As in *Independence Day*, the filmmakers originally hoped to use a variety of effect techniques to create Godzilla.

"It's the ultimate monster movie. We hope to push the limits of all the visual effects available. The technology is changing every year and in every movie we use new tools. In many ways, this film was actually more complicated than *Independence Day*. It's a huge undertaking, but after that movie, we pretty much collected all the great artists and formed our own little visual effects unit (Centropolis Effects) to help bring this creature to life," Roland Emmerich notes.

"It's the kind of movie that plays to our strengths," adds Executive Producer Ute Emmerich. "We are very comfortable with films that involve a lot of different kinds of visual and mechanical effects and this gives us an opportunity to explore that to an even greater degree."

As in *Independence Day*, the filmmakers used shot-specific effects, including miniatures, animatronic models, and computer generated images. However, as the production progressed, it became clear that CGI provided the best means by which to conjure up the new beast.

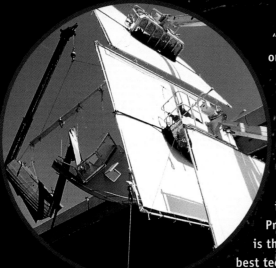

"In *Independence Day*, we went on a shot-by-shot basis, which meant we filmed things as simple as planes on a wire in front of a moving backdrop to in-camera explosions composited with live-action footage to the most complicated computer effects imaginable," notes Executive Producer Bill Fay. "Our philosophy is the same on *Godzilla*, to use the best technique for the best result. What we found was that the results we got from CG animation was technically so great that it allowed us to do things with Godzilla that we couldn't duplicate with the other processes."

The computer-generated Godzilla may have been the best way to create the sleek, swift, powerful creature that Emmerich and Devlin had envisioned, but Emmerich, Devlin, and Cinematographer Ueli Steiger did not make this easy for the animators, digital artists, and compositors.

"When we wrote *Independence Day*, we wrote it with the effects in mind," Devlin says. "In *Godzilla*, we didn't do that. We wrote it and shot it as if Godzilla was a paid actor on set. In this one, Roland had a completely free camera and later he said to Centropolis Effects, 'Figure it out.' And they did," Devlin remarks.

"The main improvement in CG was tracking. If you look at

■ TOP LEFT: *The 1/6th-scale truck being placed in front of blank screen for scene in which Godzilla attacks the Fulton Fish Market.*

■ BOTTOM LEFT: *Another view of the truck miniature model as final preparations are completed.*

■ BOTTOM LEFT TO RIGHT: *Storyboard sequence showing the plan for the truck attack.*

■ INSET RIGHT: *A view of the suspended truck cab for the live action portion of the Fulton Fish Market attack (with reflective screens placed near the suspended cab.)*

■ RIGHT TOP TO BOTTOM: *Preparations for Godzilla's attack on the truck at the Fulton Fish Market. (a) Camera track in place. (b) Positioning the truck cab. (c) Stunt truck cab hanging from a crane. (d) Light-reflecting screens through which can be seen shadows of the crane and the dangling truck cab.*

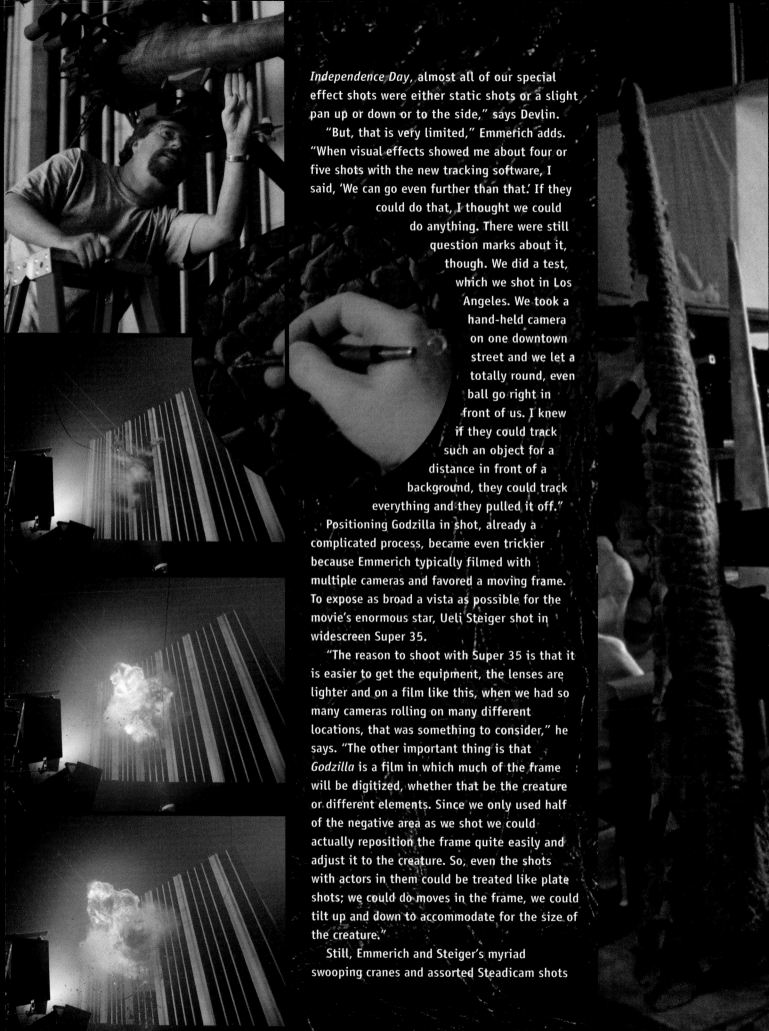

*Independence Day*, almost all of our special effect shots were either static shots or a slight pan up or down or to the side," says Devlin.

"But, that is very limited," Emmerich adds. "When visual effects showed me about four or five shots with the new tracking software, I said, 'We can go even further than that.' If they could do that, I thought we could do anything. There were still question marks about it, though. We did a test, which we shot in Los Angeles. We took a hand-held camera on one downtown street and we let a totally round, even ball go right in front of us. I knew if they could track such an object for a distance in front of a background, they could track everything and they pulled it off."

Positioning Godzilla in shot, already a complicated process, became even trickier because Emmerich typically filmed with multiple cameras and favored a moving frame. To expose as broad a vista as possible for the movie's enormous star, Ueli Steiger shot in widescreen Super 35.

"The reason to shoot with Super 35 is that it is easier to get the equipment, the lenses are lighter and on a film like this, when we had so many cameras rolling on many different locations, that was something to consider," he says. "The other important thing is that *Godzilla* is a film in which much of the frame will be digitized, whether that be the creature or different elements. Since we only used half of the negative area as we shot we could actually reposition the frame quite easily and adjust it to the creature. So, even the shots with actors in them could be treated like plate shots; we could do moves in the frame, we could tilt up and down to accommodate for the size of the creature."

Still, Emmerich and Steiger's myriad swooping cranes and assorted Steadicam shots did not make things easy for the visual effects team, which was responsible for inserting an equally kinetic creature into the film. Until recently, it was very difficult to put a moving, digital creature into a moving frame.

"In films from ten to twenty years ago, a lot of effect shots had to be done with a locked-off camera," Visual Effects Supervisor Engel explains. "It's easy to put a creature in a locked-off frame but to make the creature move together with the frame, that's the hard part. In every single frame, you not only have to move the creature itself but also lock it into the background, so it's not shifting in front of the background. Fortunately, we have good tracking software available, so that makes it much easier. We couldn't have done it a couple years ago," Engel says.

The filmmaker and the effects team initially thought the creation of the creature would be equally divided between keyframe computer animation, a system called motion-capture and animatronic creature effects. VisionArt, a house working in tandem with Centropolis Effects, was hired to provide the motion-capture and worked closely with Roland Emmerich, Patrick Tatopoulos, and Volker Engel prior to principal photography to hone the motion-capture version of the beast. Motion-capture is a system whereby electrodes attached to a human's body send signals to the computer that encodes, or "captures" this individual's movement. Once inside the computer, it can manipulate data, which, in theory, was to be assigned to Godzilla and offspring. Several talented dancers and gymnasts were hired to mimic Godzilla's movements in motion-capture and the beauty of the process was that it enabled Emmerich to "direct" an effect in real-time. As filming progressed, however, it became clear that motion-capture was just too limiting.

"Motion-capture helped us a lot (in the beginning) to define what Godzilla did. But key frame animation is one thing and motion-capture is another thing and it doesn't mix. It's too different. What we ended up doing was key-

■ FAR LEFT TOP: *Pyrotechnical expert Joe Viskocil prepares an 1/8th-scale Apache helicopter for its explosive impact into a miniature building, after it got clawed by Godzilla.*

■ FAR LEFT BOTTOM SEQUENCE: *The Apache helicopter model gets dragged into the building sitting on a long metal pole. The pole later gets removed via digital retouching.*

■ INSET LEFT: *Careful detail work creates an authentic look and feel for Godzilla's skin.*

■ LEFT: *A tail model near completion.*

■ RIGHT TOP TO BOTTOM: *Painstaking efforts at every stage of creation and construction help create a convincing reality to Godzilla's appearance.*

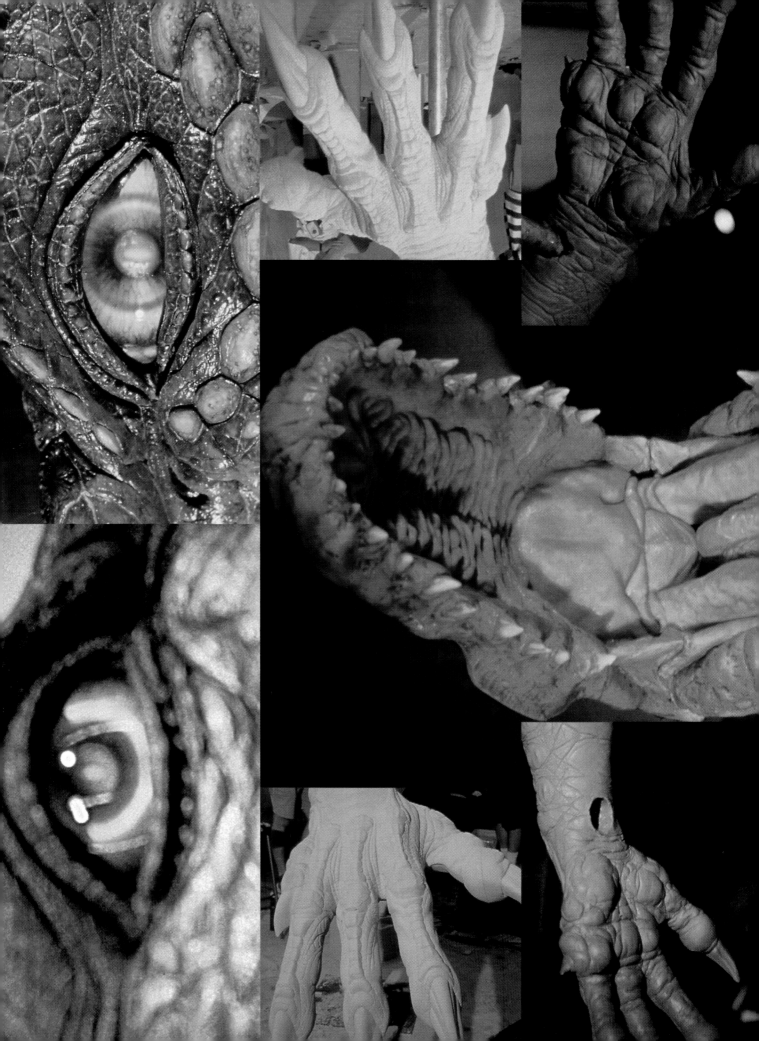

the first place?' This doesn't mean that motion-capture doesn't work, it just wasn't the right tool to animate the creature in this movie. The limitation was an undeniable human motion we couldn't get rid of," Engel explains. "With keyframe animation, we were totally free with Godzilla's movement. He could really move like a lizard."

Another technique Emmerich, Devlin, Engel and company employed was the use of animatronic models of Godzilla. After Toho approved Tatopoulos's maquette, he and his creature shop, full of sculptors, painters, model and mold makers, designed and built several different versions of Godzilla and offspring. As in *Independence Day*, the film team employed animatronic models in varying sizes, from a 1/6th-scale model to a 1/24th-scale. These mechanized representations, their facial and body movements remotely controlled, were 1/6 and 1/24 the size of the actual creature. The 1/6th-scale and 1/24th-scale Godzillas corresponded with proportionally scaled miniature buildings.

"For interaction with the models, we built a 1/6th-scale head, torso and arms, for close-ups of the creature," Patrick Tatopoulos explains. "The reason we built it that big is not because you need to make it enormous but because the model it is interacting with had to be that large to make it look real. You don't get all the right detail in the (miniature) building or helicopter unless it is 1/6th-scale, so we based the head on that."

The 1/24th-scale creature or pieces thereof, also corresponded to the modern version of Godzilla-as-guy-in-a-suit. This incarnation was not the lumbering monster of the past, but trained puppeteers, many with backgrounds in dance or performing; veterans of such sci-fi films as *Alien Resurrection* and *Mimic*, where they played glistening, deadly aliens and predatory cockroaches.

Both the 1/24th-scale and 1/6th-scale creatures were used primarily for Godzilla's disastrous physical encounters with the urban landscape.

"In looking at each shot, we're always trying to figure out, the best way to execute it successfully. What the CG creature doesn't do very well is bust through walls and chomp stuff," says Visual Effects Producer Terry Clotiaux, another *ID4* veteran. "When it had to interact with other environments, when you have to see the result of it interacting with another physical item, that was much more difficult to do in the computer."

Even so, Bill Fay notes, the effects team married much more computer work to the classic model effects than expected.

"Even in those cases that would seem to be a natural for animatronics, we sometimes used CG. There was one scene where Godzilla's chin scoops down and smashes into a roadway and we did part of it in CG because the motion of that swooping down was something we couldn't really get with animatronics. We even added digital rain to the practical rain. We discovered that a combination of the two really works best and gives a consistent look," says Fay.

To achieve this combination, Clotiaux had to supervise the filming of several practical elements to composite into the computer creations, as in *Independence Day*. Because the majority of Godzilla is shrouded in rain and the wreckage kicked up in Godzilla's wake, Clotiaux's visual effects department had to match those elements established on the first unit shoot and add them to the computer-generated world. This was a complicated proposition.

"The complexity of shots in visual effects is often based on the number of elements involved in the composite or in the visual effects shot. What we had in this project was a lot of performances dependent on visual effects work, meaning that we had the creature, we had various elements and they all interacted within the photography, so timing was crucial if the illusion was to be achieved," Clotiaux explains. "On *Independence*

■ LEFT TOP AND BOTTOM: *Detail work is done to perfect the look of the head and neck of a Godzilla model. (b) The 1/24th-scale Godzilla model is positioned in preparation for a test shoot of the destruction of some buildings during the showdown of the movie. (c) The 1/24th-scale Godzilla during the same test. For this shot, the creature was later replaced by the CG Godzilla.*

■ RIGHT: *Model maker John Hess doing final wet-down for a shot of Godzilla breaking through the pavement of a model street.*

■ ABOVE: (a) The Zeiss measuring tool. (b) VFX Supervisor Volker Engel on the Park Avenue set with the Godzilla match-move team. (c) The match-move specialists in New York: Joe Jackman, John Schmidt and Archie Gogoladze.

■ INSET: Match-move specialist John Schmidt who became the maestro of the Zeiss measuring tool.

*Day*, we had the luxury of making all the different gags come together in compositing. In this movie, we dealt with a lot more stuff that was in-camera and very critical — the creature, smoke, rain, rain, RAIN, debris. All those elements were not separate pieces that could be composited together later. They had to interact together just right, at exactly the same moment."

To keep track of all these components, the effects department relied on a software program invented on *Independence Day*.

"For visual effects, organization is key. Once we broke down a shot into its different elements, we used a highly sophisticated data base program called 'Dave.' It was developed during *Independence Day* to help us track our information. Like any project that involves many teams, communication and the passing of information between those teams was critical. Our job was to make sure that as information changed, as new stuff was added or deleted, all that got updated and distributed to the appropriate people. In fact, we had a professional data wrangler, Tricia Mulgrew, and that was her whole job, just handling the information. Everything was in one system and the idea

## WE COULD MATHEMATICALLY FIGURE OUT WHERE THE CAMERA WAS, BASED ON RECONCILING BETWEEN THE 3-D AND 2-D INFORMATION.

was that once it got entered, it was available to the digital department making the creature, it was available to editorial...everything from camera angle to lenses, everything that had to do with that shot was in the data base."

Clotiaux notes that many times, the visual effects shot was completed "without the benefit of our star." In fact, Godzilla was almost the last thing to be added because he was often a completely computer-generated creature. Even so, he was always on set, with the first unit team. Once he appeared as several large green barrels serving as "foot holders" at the Fulton Fish Market, where the digital artists would later insert his menacing taloned toes. Most of the time, he sent his surrogates, three skinny guys

carrying a pole with a reflector on its end, a video camera and a surveying tool poised on a tripod. This odd assortment of equipment helped "data wranglers" Joe Jackman, John Schmidt and Archie Gogoladze, under Visual Effects Supervisor Volker Engel's guidance, plot Godzilla's presence.

"In order to put Godzilla in the movie," Engel explains "we had to know where the camera was in every frame. To do that, we figured out where everything was by actually taking 3-D measurements of everything and then comparing that to the 2-D information in the frame. We could mathematically figure out where the camera was, based on reconciling between the 3-D and 2-D information.

"The Zeiss counter helped us do that," he continues. "It's a piece of surveying equipment, pretty much the best in the world, and it was essential for measuring in New York City because we had all these tall buildings."

The buildings, coupled with Godzilla's enormous size, obviated the more typical mode of tracking a digital creature in space, Z-tracking. This process usually involves the use of a sphere and a cube, objects the computer recognizes, in terms of spatial orientation. Clearly, this was much too puny a method to measure something like Godzilla.

"What we did was to utilize a tracking system, using this Zeiss surveying tool, so we could create a CG (computer graphic) environment in which we have all these points where the buildings actually are and we can put the creature into this CG world," Engel explains. "The Zeiss tool is essentially an architectural measuring device; you know exactly where the buildings are, what their altitude is, where

exactly you have to place Godzilla so he can move down the street. That helped us a lot, because we were dealing with this gigantic creature, so we couldn't use the standard Z-tracking. Nobody has really ever dealt with a creature this size in a CG environment before," Engel explains.

Jackman adds that they used the pole with the reflector to compensate for the buildings' odd angles. "Sometimes if the side of a building was really oblique, we'd take the pole to it because otherwise it would bounce away from us. With the reflector, we got a bounce back from the building."

The Hi–8 camera gave some shape to the data collected with the pole and the Zeiss tracking tool and the information went from New York to the visual effects unit in Los Angeles via the Web. "We'd videotape each point so we didn't just have a file with a bunch of numbers, we knew what they were," Jackman says. "Then we'd capture frames off the video into the laptop, add text and arrows and stuff, indicate the point number and send it back to the office on the Internet. The data got uploaded to a protected website where visual effects had access."

Because Godzilla's "performance" was so integrated into a majority of the first unit scenes, especially those shot in New York, Volker Engel was also a constant presence on the set. His arrival meant that Godzilla or his progeny were somewhere in the scene.

"In *Godzilla* I was involved with the first unit early on and was there pretty much during the whole live-action shoot, especially on location, to make sure we could get the shots in such a way so we could put Godzilla in later. On *Independence Day*, I wasn't involved with much of the principal photography. This time, we had to put the creature in most of the shots and one-half to two-thirds of the movie's visual effects are live-action shots that require the creature. So, my job was much more integrated with the first unit shooting," Engel says. "A normal shooting day in New York would be like this: Climb into a shaking helicopter at five in the morning to supervise an aerial sequence, rush to the main unit set to discuss the shots with Roland, spend the night with the second unit to supervise the motion-control shoot of empty streets, rush to the airport to fly to L.A. to a meeting with Terry (Clotiaux) to plan the shoot of the miniatures."

Although the film's eponymous star was never actually on set, Emmerich always directed with him in mind. This meant fashioning actions and reactions, from screaming crowds to crashing cars, as if this giant menace was on set. It also required careful camera positioning so that the visual effects department could add Godzilla later.

"It's all about how the shot gets blocked so that in the end you're actually able to put Godzilla in there; the camera can't just point down the street because Godzilla is twenty stories high."

Additionally, Emmerich had to stage sequences so that they could be matched later with models of Godzilla-pulverized buildings or computer images, ranging from the creature to a fleet of helicopters giving chase through Manhattan. With his extensive experience in all kinds of effects techniques, in many ways, *Godzilla* and Emmerich were a perfect match.

"One of the many great things about working with Roland is that he already knows when he shoots his live-

■ LEFT TOP: *The 1/6th-scale creature bites into the fish truck.*

■ LEFT BOTTOM: *The scene was shot against a painted sky backdrop.*

■ RIGHT TOP: *Model Maker, Kirk Yamashita, works on the Flatiron Building's mechanical rig.*

■ INSET: *Miniature Flatiron Building on set the day of filming.*

■ RIGHT BOTTOM: *A live-action shot of the real Flatiron Building.*

action portion of the film, how he will put the effects in, which helps me do my job," says Engel. "At the same time, he's a good communicator and has a very definite idea about the look he wants. You don't end up trying things out five different times because Roland is sure how he wants the shot to look."

While Emmerich, Devlin and company worked through the nights in New York, the nascent digital Godzilla began to take shape in Los Angeles. Tatopoulos worked closely with the computer wizards at Centropolis Effects, to exactly establish the creature's movements and to synchronize them with those of the animatronic models.

"At that point, there was nothing in the computer yet, just a scan of the creature based on the maquette," Tatopoulos says. "I thought it was important to work both with the mechanical effects department, which was making the animatronic models, as well as with the CG designers to maintain some consistency, (in terms of) the textures, the colors and, movement. I wanted to make sure the character was rendered in the computer to exactly match our original concept, which actually took a long period of time, three or four months. I also wanted to ensure that the character was moving properly, in the same pattern as Roland and I had discussed. So, I worked with the CG and mechanical effects crews, using the same reference base to choreograph the creature's movements."

These CG designers, particularly Centropolis Effects' CG supervisors Steffen Wild and Carolin Quis, communicated Tatopoulos's desires and instructions ultimately to a company called Viewpoint DataLabs. Steven Puri, the head of Centropolis Effects which would spearhead the

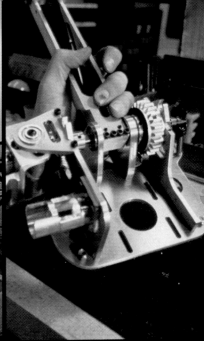

computer work, had contracted the Utah-based Viewpoint DataLabs to design the digital model.

"Viewpoint is a company that specializes in creating custom datasets for computer graphics use," Puri explains. "A lot of people at Centropolis Effects have worked with Viewpoint when they were at different effects houses and I'd worked extensively with them for a long time. We actually talked at Siggraph a few years ago about how cool it would be to build Godzilla in a computer-generated form. We finally had the chance to do it."

In fact, Viewpoint DataLabs had begun work on *Godzilla*, in its earlier incarnation, when Jan De Bont was set to direct the picture. Walter Noot, Viewpoint's vice-president of production, soon discovered that his company's previous *Godzilla* research and development was now obsolete.

"Sony Imageworks was thinking about doing it for awhile and we were involved in building the creature for them, which was really based on the original look. So that

■ TOP FROM LEFT TO RIGHT: *(a) Creature specialist Jake Garber does some touch-up work on the 1/6th-scale Godzilla between takes. (b-h) Various views of the mechanical parts that come together for the Baby Godzilla man-in-suit models: (b) Front view of body frame. (c) Padded interior support frame for performer. (d) Side view of body frame. (e) Performer wearing padded shoulder harness with Baby Godzilla head. (f) Two tails with internal bungee cords. (g) Construction frame for a larger Godzilla model. (h) Part of the mechanism for creating movement.*

■ LEFT: *Godzilla actor Kurt Carley gets dressed for one of his performances.*

■ INSET: *Godzilla actor Kurt Carley pauses between takes.*

■ INSET: *Creature designer Patrick Tatopoulos discusses an upcoming shot with Kurt Carley who played Godzilla wherever the "man-in-suit" technique was used.*

was cool, we built that and we had some other experiences building Godzilla models, so we were pretty excited to get involved with this production. We were really surprised to see what the creature looked like, when we saw it for the first time, because there was a lot of secrecy around seeing it. After signing all our agreements and signing our lives and families away, we got a creature about two feet high and we actually marked that up and digitized that model so that they could start working on making the creature come alive. It started changing pretty quickly," explains Noot.

Indeed, Tatopoulos's design began to shift slightly, as the filmmakers decided to discard some of its more anthropomorphic features for more reptilian ones. Also, about this time, the 1/24th-scale suits were nearly ready. It seemed logical to lend one of those beasts to Viewpoint for digitizing.

"Patrick and his team started making changes. They still needed to put a guy in a suit and that hadn't really been put into the design of the character and all at once a lot of the proportions of the creature started changing and on top of that, the creature started changing artistically and then we got another version of junior. Then they decided here at Centropolis Effects to have us actually digitize a large scale version of it, so we actually got the big one that the guy stands in. What had happened was that once they had gone through two generations of

creative review, they decided to resculpt and recast the whole, both the baby and the mother version, junior and senior and that's when we got those models," Noot recalls.

He adds that when the 1/24th-scale creature arrived, his team was as astonished as if a 400-foot lizard had suddenly appeared in Utah.

"Then we saw the monster, the big 1/24th-scale monster. That was a real monster to us, digitizing that thing and modeling it, it was just really an intense monster. There were a lot of modelers that we had outside of Viewpoint, just working on that thing. Day to day, working on the computer and really working on not just looking at the entire creature, but looking at just little individual pieces, the scales of this creature, to make sure they all lined up and everything looked really perfect," Noot says.

Because the creature was so immense and detailed, digitizing it became a bit like the fable about the blind man and the elephant; each modeler took

■ LEFT INSET: *A wireframe view of the CG Godzilla head created by Viewpoint Data Labs.*

■ LOWER LEFT: *A Godzilla skeleton model.*

■ TOP: *A wireframe profile view of the CG Godzilla.*

■ ABOVE: *A wireframe top view of the CG Godzilla.*

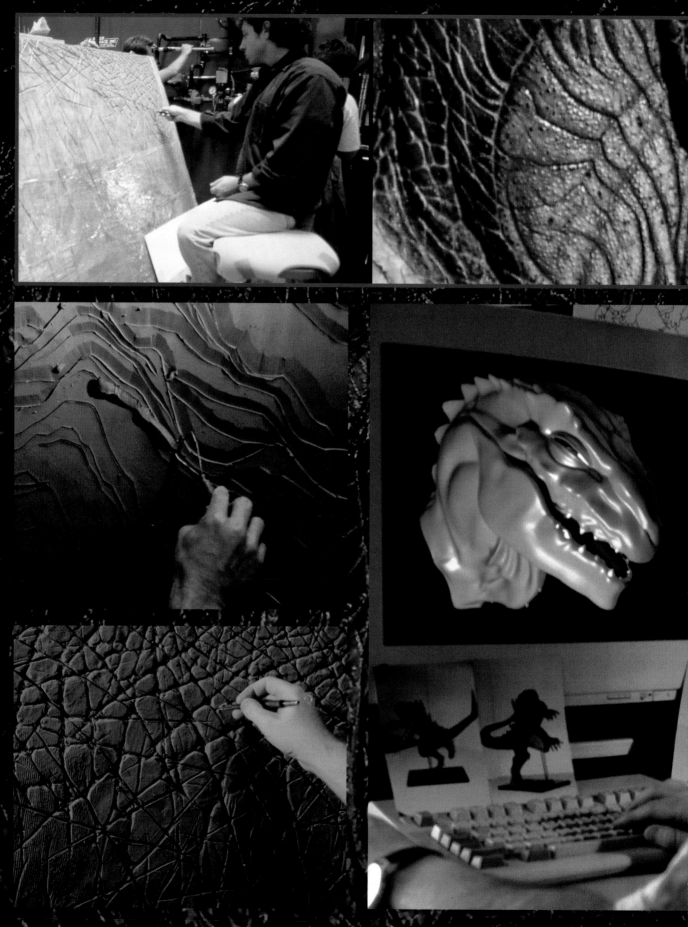

a different part, but no one had a
clear view of the entire creature.

"We had the models, the
1/24th-scale models, we
actually marked it up with a
pen and then we had an arm
that had like a stylus attached
to it and we digitized each plane
like that. So, some of it, you can
imagine little tiny, tiny polygons
you can barely even see are marked
around this little scale or something.
And the mark up jobs on these were just
incredible. Sometimes the digitizing was so
intense, it was I think the most intense creature we've ever digitized, because it's
so big, there's so much detail, so many little pieces. The sculptors just went wild on
it, all the scales and bumps, our digitizers went crazy. We had people working
around the clock digitizing this thing, different parts. You know, one guy would
have a leg, another would have a tail and they'd be digitizing away," Noot explains.
"The head, oh man, the head was intense . . . the teeth, every single tooth, the
eyes, the larynx . . ."

At one point, Noot says up to ten modelers were toiling away, which, he points
out, is highly unusual for a single creature. "Standard issue for a film . . . well,
*Batman* was about five or six modelers and those are big films, those are all the
characters in that. This is ONE character, that's what's different about it," Noot says.

The process became even more complicated because Centropolis Effects and
VisionArt, the two companies initially working on the computer-animated Godzilla,
favored two different systems.

Noot explains, "We had a few different kinds of models that we had to build
because we had two production houses involved. CFX is working on it and so is
VisionArt. VisionArt is using a polygonal model and CFX is using a NURBS (non-
uniform rational B-spline component) model."

When Viewpoint finished its labors, CGI Supervisors Carolin Quis and Steffen

■ OPPOSITE PAGE NEAR LEFT: *A CG
screen shot of Godzilla's head with skin
surface in place, awaiting texture layering.*

■ TOP LEFT TO RIGHT: *(a) An artist
works on details of skin texture for an
animatronic model. (b) Close-up view of
skin detail. (c) Another view of skin tex-
turing. (d) Close-up of the skin folds at
the neck of a Godzilla model.*

■ LEFT MIDDLE: *Roughing out the skin
texture.*

■ LEFT BOTTOM: *Creating the fine details
of three-dimensional texture of the skin
for the Godzilla models.*

■ INSET: *Detail of Godzilla model jaw
showing beginnings of neck skin folds.*

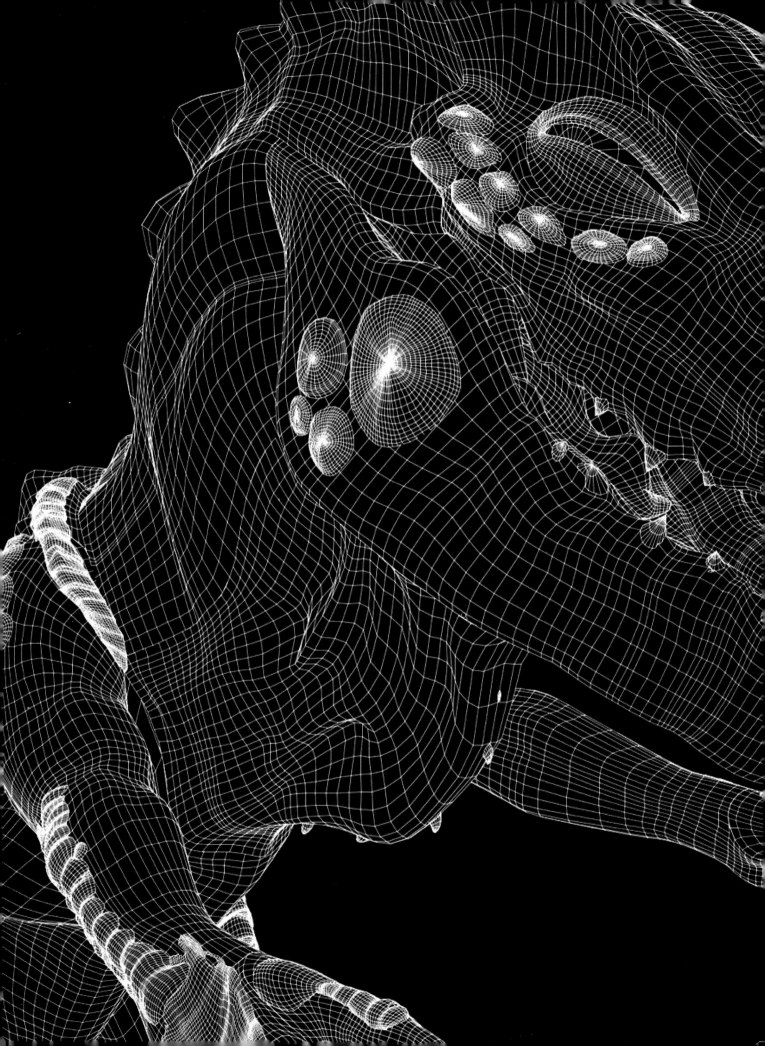

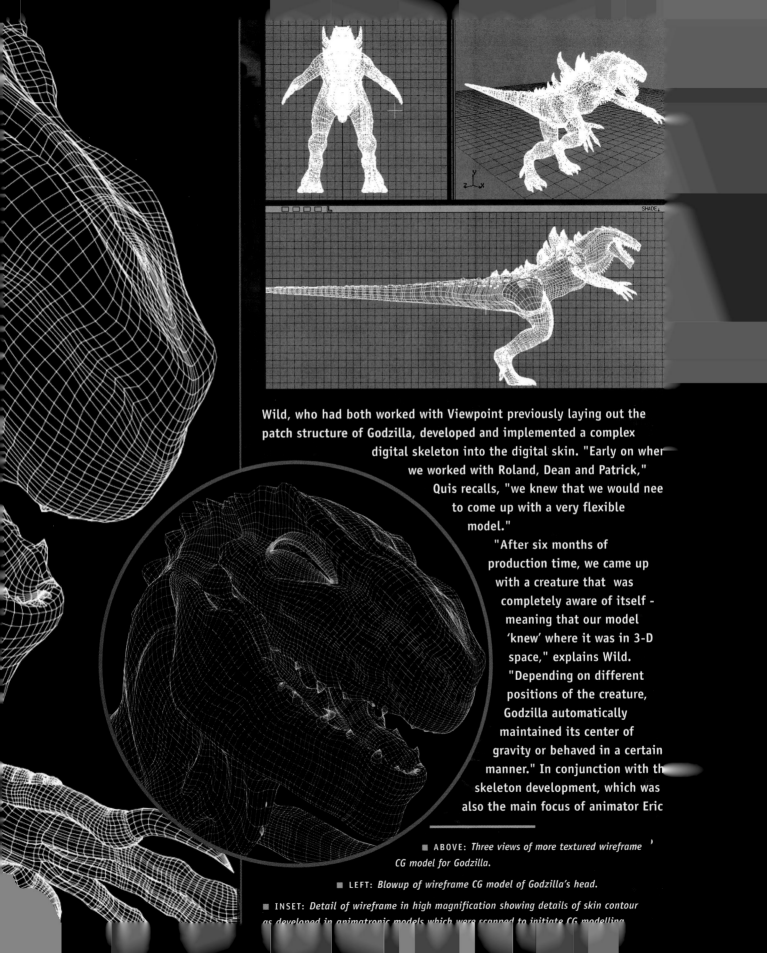

Wild, who had both worked with Viewpoint previously laying out the patch structure of Godzilla, developed and implemented a complex digital skeleton into the digital skin. "Early on when we worked with Roland, Dean and Patrick," Quis recalls, "we knew that we would need to come up with a very flexible model."

"After six months of production time, we came up with a creature that was completely aware of itself - meaning that our model 'knew' where it was in 3-D space," explains Wild. "Depending on different positions of the creature, Godzilla automatically maintained its center of gravity or behaved in a certain manner." In conjunction with the skeleton development, which was also the main focus of animator Eric

■ ABOVE: *Three views of more textured wireframe CG model for Godzilla.*

■ LEFT: *Blowup of wireframe CG model of Godzilla's head.*

■ INSET: *Detail of wireframe in high magnification showing details of skin contour as developed in animatronic models which were scanned to initiate CG modelling.*

Weiss, lead texture artist Robin Higgin-Foley came up with highly detailed textures for the monster using 3-D paint software such as Amazon 3-D paint. "The turnaround time for one shot from the start of the animation through the lighting and rendering phase and up to the final composite was a big issue," says Quis. "To minimize the time to light the creature, we rendered Godzilla with white lights and created mattes—black and white

**TOP ROW:** *(a) Digital Effects Producer Fiona Bull in her command center. She managed to steer the digital ship and its crew even through the stormiest logistical seas. (b) CG Supervisors Steffen Wild and Carolin Quis developed the computer-generated Godzilla. More than ninety percent of the creature in the movie is done CG. (c) Conny Fauser-Ruemelin, who had created a lot of the well-known images in the movie Independence Day, is one of the Compositing Supervisors. VFX-Supervisor Volker Engel gives some input for one of the shots. (d) From left to right: Joe Jackman, Lead Matchmove Artist; Steffen Wild, CG Supervisor; Karen Goulekas, Associate Visual Effects Supervisor; Carolyn Quis, CG Supervisor. (e) John Lewis, the head of Research and Development, helped solve even the toughest software problems.*

**SECOND ROW:** *(a) Compositing Supervisor Conny Fauser-Ruemelin is incorporating some strong light beams, so called "god-rays" into a compositing shot of the Brooklyn Bridge. (b) Lead Texture Artist Robin Higgin-Foley became the specialist for Godzilla's skin. (c) Technical Director Michael Sean Foley works on the shot in which Godzilla steps over New York's FDR Drive. (d) Together with Animation Supervisor Andy Jones (who animated fifty percent of the Godzilla shots in the movie), Alice Kaiserian animated the creature in most of the chase sequence at the end of the movie.*

**THIRD ROW:** *(a) Compositing Artist Scott Holmes in a rare suicide attempt with a plastic toy gun. (b) Lead Lighting Artist Frederic Soumagnas discusses the lighting for a CG shot with Daniel Fazel, one of the technical directors. (c) Baby Godzilla Animator Jay Randall. (d) Hiding in his corner we see Baby Godzilla-Lead-Animator Matt Hackett. He brought Godzilla's brood to life.*

**FOURTH ROW:** *(a) CG Animator Eric Weiss animated Godzilla's head and claw reaching inside the Park Avenue tunnel. CG Supervisor Steffen Wild, Associate Visual Effects (b) Supervisor Karen Goulekas and Daniel Fazel, one of the Technical Directors, are discussing a shot at one of the Silicon Graphics workstations at Centropolis Effects. (c) Compositing Artists Abra Grupp and Mario Peixoto (standing) in a rather funny discussion with VFX Supervisor Volker Engel who examines a toy dinosaur. (d) Animation Supervisor Andy Jones at his computer, on which he created the animations for more than fifty percent of the Godzilla shots. (e) Associate Visual Effects Supervisor Karen Goulekas was the driving force during the digital postproduction of the movie. Here she discusses a shot with Compositing Supervisor Mitch Drain.*

images—for each of the lights in the scene. This way, the final lighting of the creature which was headed up by lead lighting artist Frederic Soumagnas could be controlled up to the very last minute by Roland and Volker and Karen in the compositing process, but we still had to contend with the enormous amount of work required to make the creature appear agile."

"After we had worked out everything within the creature," Wild says, "we tackled the tasks around the creature. Our in-house development group headed up by John Lewis helped us streamline the rendering process and get our creature from Softimage into Houdini where we did all our effects work."

"Every time the creature takes a step, it leaves a serious impact on the surface behind," adds Quis. "With the effects team led by Sean Cunningham we were able to offer Roland the freedom to create digital debris, rain and pavement cracks in all the shots we did at CFX."

"But as soon as we thought we had everything under control," Wild recalls,"Roland asked us to come up with a similar pipeline for the Baby Godzillas as well. Luckily, what took us six months of development for Godzilla, took us only 6 weeks for the babies."

"This skeleton would 'drive' the skin during animation," Steven Puri explains. "We used several different software packages to do this: Soft Image's 3-D animation system was used for all key frame animation of the creature at CFX. At the same time, VisionArt was creating a matching skeleton that would allow them to animate in Side Effects 3-D animation system prisms."

Slowly, the computerized creature began to progress. Next, the CG skin had to attain its texture and hue, albeit within the parameters of computer software and hardware.

"In order to render the creature, the CG skin had to be 'painted' or 'textured.' This process associates the points on the skin with a color value that is then applied when the CG creature is rendered," says Steffen Wild.

Most of this technology was available through advanced software. However, because the creature and its new look and abilities was so complex, one or two over-the-counter software packages were insufficient. In fact, Soft Image lent its Special Projects team to *Godzilla* to overcome some of the software's limitations.

■ INSET: *A CG Godzilla showing full body with arms spread and tail extended – a perfect view of the New Godzilla in his highly mobile glory.*

# SLOWLY, THE COMPUTERIZED CREATURES BEGAN TO PROGRESS. NEXT THE CG SKIN HAD TO ATTAIN ITS TEXTURE AND HUE.

"None of the software is perfect. That's the thing that's so hard about this industry. The reason animators and artists are in such high demand is that the tools are very hard to learn. You have to have the talent to be able to use them and to try to figure out what the advantages or disadvantages of the tools are," Wild says. "That's what we dealt with here. We were working with these software packages and really pushing them to the limit. Soft Image actually came out, with their Special Projects team, and worked very closely and directly with us to try to solve some of the problems with animation and skinning tools, because we were trying to do things that haven't been done before. It's all R&D. It's almost like you need a whole R&D team to investigate the tools because you're always pushing the barriers," Puri says.

One of the breakthroughs this joint research and development achieved was a program written by Imageware, contracted by Soft Image's Special Projects. This program helped make Godzilla's skin seamless, a crucial development, since the fabric-like NURB surface inevitably leads to a "seam" in the skin.

■ BOTTOM LEFT TO RIGHT: *(a) A supply of finished Godzilla model body parts ready to be shipped from Model Shop. (b) Model Shop workers doing final assembly on a smaller model. (c) Another view of workers doing final body assembly. (d) Detail work being done on the jaw for a small-scale model.*

With its pliant skeleton and an approximation of its textured skin, the creature was ready to move. This required the inventive skills of more than twenty computer graphic artists at CFX, working with Emmerich and Engel over an eighteen-month period. Those artists working on the film increased as the computer work did. Fortunately, about the time the filmmakers realized that they would need more animators, digital artists, and compositors, many of them became available. Previously, many had worked at Jim Cameron's Digital Domain, on his epic *Titanic*. They completed their work around the time the computer effects in *Godzilla* began to expand. Karen Goulekas, a Digital Domain expatriate, joined the *Godzilla* team as associate visual effects supervisor and several of her Digital Domain colleagues followed her.

"I'd spent the last four years at Digital Domain. The last show I did was *The Fifth Element*, as digital effects supervisor. Before that, I was the DFX supervisor on *Apollo 13*, *T2 3-D* and *Strange Days*. Right after *Fifth*, they promoted me to visual effects supervisor and I was involved in breaking down and building on about fifteen different shows—many of which weren't even green-lit. So, after four frustrating months, I figured I'd look around. If they came up with a really cool project for me, fine, I'd stick around. If not, I'd keep looking. I was specifically looking for a character show, because I had done the photo-real shows, like *Apollo* and *True Lies* and I had specifically taken *Fifth* because it was out there and artsy. After that, I wanted a mix of live-action and a character show. I didn't want anything to do with *Godzilla*, because it was in the middle of shooting and I had come into *Apollo 13* in the middle of that show and I told myself I'd never do that again. But, if there was another character-driven show in the works..."

Instead, Puri told Goulekas that they

were, in fact, looking for a digital effects supervisor. Initially, Goulekas balked, but they offered her an elevated title and besides, Goulekas thought *Godzilla* would be a relatively simple task at this late stage in production.

"I thought that coming in that late in the game, I couldn't make a lot of the software development decisions that a visual effects supervisor would make up front. I figured I'd just inherit it and it would be more about just getting the stuff to look good."

In fact, Goulekas overhauled the entire digital system. She tripled the staff of artists, bringing in a digital effects team to make digital rain, debris, and smoke and expanding the animating staff. She rejected the prism rendering software package in favor of Soft Image's Mental Ray system, suggested corrections to certain networking and facility pipeline problems, and eliminated the motion-capture technique entirely. Under her guidance, Godzilla migrated almost entirely into the computer.

■ ABOVE: *Miniature Effects Supervisor Don Baker sets up a shot that will include tanks firing at Godzilla when he jumps into the Hudson River.*

■ LEFT: *First Assistant VFX-cameraman Jeff Sturgill amongst the buildings of the street that Godzilla chooses to make his escape towards the Hudson River.*

# GOULEKAS OVERHAULED THE ENTIRE DIGITAL SYSTEM. SHE TRIPLED THE STAFF OF ARTISTS.

The irony of directing a computer-derived Godzilla was not lost on Emmerich, who is a confessed computer neophyte. However, the incredible range of articulation and expression the computer afforded his huge star also allowed the director to take the film in directions he couldn't have considered without it. Goulekas adds that she found Emmerich to be a giving and supportive advocate of her work.

ABOVE: *Shot of the full-scale jaws crushing a cab.*

OPPOSITE PAGE TOP: *Working on the soundstage to set up the full-scale Godzilla jaws.*

OPPOSITE PAGE BOTTOM: *Machinery for operating the full-scale Godzilla jaws.*

"What I liked best about working with Roland was that he was so open. There is always this question about when do you show it to the director? When is it too late, when have you gone down a path that you shouldn't have and that's not what the director wanted because you misunderstood, and when is it too soon, so that he gets frustrated. Every morning, we looked at the dailies to decide what we could show Roland, but I found him to be really open to letting us change things. I felt really comfortable saying stuff like, 'You know what, Roland? This isn't working. Can we slide the plate? Is it okay if we repo(sition) the plate? Can we change the action?' He had to cut the sequences with blank plates, so what I like best about character animation is that we could re-create the cut, for various reasons. If we needed to lengthen it because there wasn't enough time to do the action or if we had to shorten it because we were killing time for the action. And Roland was really responsive to that, even if, once and awhile, I got it totally wrong."

One of the most daunting tasks facing Goulekas's team of computer animators was how to translate the creature's predatory nature, its twitchy lizard-like tics, its reptilian inscrutability and its sinuous, feline power into movement. Andy Jones, fresh off *Titanic*, was the animator who captured it.

"In terms of the artists approaching animating Godzilla and finding the right guy for the job, it's like casting a role. It really is, it's completely an artistic endeavor. When Andy cracked it, Roland said, 'Andy's Godzilla.' And that's really the way it works. It's a hard thing to predict, too. I mean, one of the reasons we set it up so that we had the

ability to use more than one process (beyond CG)
is that you never know what's going to end up
working," notes Bill Fay.

Everyone was so pleased with Jones's efforts
that they promoted him to animation supervisor.

"That was really nice and a big surprise," the
soft-spoken Jones says of his new title. He can't
pinpoint one defining element he brought to the
character, but cites a number of influences.

"It was a combination of a lot of things. It was
Roland's input about its agility, it was Dean's
input about speed and the need to stay away
from the original Godzilla, which was very clunky.
So, I started thinking about combining things
like an alligator —we had reference footage of
alligators, we had reference footage of creatures
running, like lions or leopards and stuff like that.
So, I looked at all of this and tried to combine
them all into one and make a creature that ran
with agility but had the fierceness and the
predatory nature of an alligator. The other thing
was that Patrick Tatopoulos was a major
influence, too, and gave me a lot of input as to
how the creature should move. He was always
mentioning that it should be very catlike and
sneak up on things the way cats do when they it
go into predator mode, like lions," Jones says.

Jones's gift was to take these nuances and give
them life through his talent as an animator. The
result was a marvelous combination of physics, art
and science that he cannot entirely explain.

"Basically, I just took my animation skills,
which is what I know about animation and timing
and weight and stuff like that and added that into
the creature. It took a lot of control of certain
elements. When I first got here, the model was
working really well but there were a few changes
that needed to be made to the way they were
animating it. So, we made those changes in a lot of
the animation. For instance, we tried out a new
hip translation because every time we moved the
feet, the head kind of stayed in between the feet.
So, we couldn't get the full weight and texture, it
was very rigid every time it stepped, it was very
abrupt stopping, it didn't feel very smooth. We
used that to rough out the animation and then we
got rid of it and smoothed out the entire
movement of the creature," Jones says.

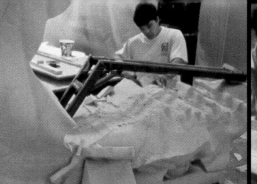

The goal, he adds, was to not only accent the creature's speed and strength, but to give it weight and mass, even in the smallest details.

"A similar process had to be gone through with the animation of th baby Godzillas'. It was animator Matt Hackett who mastered the young creatures' pack behavior and predatory movements. He was given the daunting task of heading up the group of artists who sometimes had t animate more than one hundred babies in one shot alone."

Once Godzilla and kin moved to Emmerich's liking, they had to be placed into their virtual scenes and lit, like their human counterparts on the set. Unlike their human co-stars, it often required several manifestations to create the creature, depending on the needs of the scene.

"The goal was to have the computer create an image of Godzilla or Bab Godzilla with lighting that simulated how the real environment would hav lit him," Wild explains. "Once the lights were approved, the whole scene was sent for rendering, where for each frame, an image of Godzilla or Bab Godzilla was created and stored on disc. Often, to achieve a very specific look of Godzilla in the scene, multiple images of Godzilla were rendered with slightly different surfaces. For example, a 'beauty' or 'normal' pass, a 'wet' pass, a 'matte' pass, etc., so that later in the process the artists coul mix them together in different ratios, based on the demands of the scene This allowed the compositors to retain some flexibility to match the creature into the right background plate."

Several of the high-tech machines required to achieve these various renderings lived at Centropolis Effects, mainly Silicon Graphics Challenge servers and a few Intergraph Render Rax servers. This equipment made a complex creature like Godzilla possible.

Once the character animation had been approved by Emmerich, the animation files were rendered with textures and lighting at Centropolis Effects, Sony Imageworks and VisionArt. Ninety per cent of the animation had been done by the artists at CFX, but the facility had never planned to complete as many shots as it ended up animating. Digital Effects Produce Fiona Bull worked with Goulekas and Engel in assigning shots to the vario digital houses. She and her coordinator Glenn Karpf would then ensure th the thousands upon thousands of elements needed, both practical and CG would get to the facilities in order for the shots to make their deadlines.

For that to happen, a team of compositors at Centropolis Effects, Sony

into the scenes. It was down to lead compositors such as Conny Fauser-Ruenrelin, Mitchell Drain and Nelson Sepulveda to make the audience believe that Godzilla was really rampaging through New York, leaving a scene of mass destruction in his wake. Many times, Emmerich had filmed a shot months before: a location vista of, for instance, the Flatiron District, containing actors, an army of extras and their military hardware and accessories— everything but Godzilla.

Once rendered, this CG image of Godzilla eventually had to be placed into scenes. A team of compositors, at Centropolis Effects, Sony Imageworks, and Digiscope contributed to this effort. At this point, all the elements, CG and practical, including Godzilla, were placed or "composited" into the background plate. Many times, Emmerich had filmed this plate shot months before, a location vista of, for instance, the Flatiron District, containing actors, an army of extras and their military hardware and accessories, everything but Godzilla.

Well, perhaps, not everything. Many of the "practical elements" that had to be added to the scene, including debris or smoke or bigger ticket items, such as exploding model buildings, were shot individually, under Volker Engel and Terry Clotiaux's guidance. All this occurred at the Playa Vista studios complex, a sprawling lot full of airplane hangars, vestiges of its former incarnation, Hughes Aircraft. This was familiar terrain for most of the crew members, as they had also filmed *Independence Day* there.

Although they filmed the same kind of pieces there for *Independence Day*, Clotiaux says that *Godzilla* was much more complicated.

"It's the fact that all these different elements were interacting together, that they weren't separate elements so that we would shoot this, shoot this, shoot this, shoot this and then go to the compositing process and put those things together. In this process, for instance, when Godzilla's moving through the subway tunnel, we had a CG creature, we have a certain smoke density established when the first unit shot the scene, we have debris falling around the creature. We had to add more debris to the shot, with just the right amount of smoke, and one piece of debris flying into the lens at an inappropriate moment and the shot is useless. So, it was the fact that we had to get them all interacting together, in-camera, which

■ ABOVE LEFT TO RIGHT:
*(a) Tail piece for the 1/6th scale Godzilla. (b) Angle view of a Model Shop workman doing early stage construction on a body part. (c) Fins and barbs (various sizes) being readied for attachment to the Godzilla model. (d) Scaffold built around 1/6th scale model during final assembly. (e) Exterior body for a Baby Godzilla showing the leg mechanism and tail in place.*

■ INSET: *Eye and eye ridge model.*

■ LEFT: *Complete leg model of the 1/6th scale Godzilla.*

made it much more difficult," Clotiaux explains.

Additionally, *Godzilla* presented Clotiaux's team with several new challenges, in the form of the animatronic models of Godzilla and babies.

"I guess the mechanical creature work was new and different for us. It was a big difference for us, in terms of working with 1/24th-scale mechanical creature pieces and the 1/6th-scale (mechanical head) that will be truly extraordinary. The mechanics of putting that together was pretty amazing, all of the machinery that was under the skin. In looking at each shot, we're always trying to figure out what is the best, of the tools we have, what's the best way to execute it successfully and the CG animation world, the things that it does best, that we can't do mechanically, are wide shots and various other things. But what it doesn't do very well is bust through walls and chomp stuff so when it has to interact with other environments, when you have to see the result of it interacting with other physical items, then it is much more difficult. So almost all the stuff that we have with mechanical creatures, had to do with it busting through a wall, hitting a wall, chomping something. We used the 1/6th-scale head mainly for close-ups."

Although some of the tight shots of Godzilla eventually ended up as CG work, the 1/6th-scale head was useful and a marvel to behold. A behemoth, technically a "miniature," it was a huge, hydraulic machine, featuring an immense face, neck and torso and could extend thirty-feet into the air. It was so big that only an airplane hangar at Hughes could house it. Radio controlled, its wiring extended up the spine and into the skull and it took three puppeteers to manipulate its various facial movements, from sneering lips, hinged jaws that opened

■ LEFT TOP: *A crewman makes some adjustments to the mechanism that controls the full-scale Godzilla jaw model.*

■ LEFT CENTER: *The Tatopoulos crew is using radio-controls to maneuver the twenty foot full-scale creature.*

■ LEFT BOTTOM: *Another view of the jaws with a cab caught between the teeth.*

■ INSET: *Shot of the full-scale jaws crushing a cab.*

■ RIGHT: *Close-up look at the interior design of the jaws for the 1/24th-scale Godzilla model.*

and shut on command and blinking eyes. Its horizontal and vertical moves emanated from a man in a glass-enclosed booth. He operated the motion-base upon which the head sat. This device, which was originally built for the theme park industry and aerospace, was a platform with six "axes of freedom," which allowed the mounted head to rise, tilt, heave, surge, and bounce from left to right. The 1/6th-scale head was so immense, though, that it required a similarly tremendous motion-base. Prior to *Godzilla*, James Cameron employed it for *True Lies*, to maneuver the film's jet fighter!

One of the Baby Godzillas also stood on a motion base, albeit a much smaller one. This was a fully-hydraulic animatronic character, from about the knees up.

"The idea behind that one was that there is certain anatomy between an actor in a suit and the actual anatomy of the creature that are never going to mesh perfectly. As far as really violent, fast and anatomically correct movement, we'd only get that from a mechanical beast, so that's what that one was for," says the creature crew's Mechanical Department Supervisor Guy Himber.

However, most of the babies were actually suits, individually tailored for specially trained puppeteers. Except for the dead ones . . .

"For the babies, we built four hero suits, which were walking suits or standing suits, whatever we wanted, with full mechanical heads, with every function. Then we built three stunt suits, which were slightly lighter, they still have eyes and mouth mechanism working. And we built two dead babies, not just to lie around . . . well, they did lie around, but we built the skeletons inside so when we grabbed the head, the full body responds, the body had motion so you can give them motion. Just moving them around, you feel the weight, they're not just like stiff dead rubber babies," Tatopoulos notes.

Additionally, the "baby suits," according to Guy Himber, featured ". . . actual working, walk-around legs as well as purely static legs."

Initially, the Baby Godzilla suits were conceived so that through the puppeteers inside them could amble around the set. To do so and to angle their legs in less-than-human positions, the puppeteers stood on small stilts build inside the suit's lower legs, which veered at about a 45-degree angle.

"Generally, when you have a shot with someone on leg extensions, they'll make those legs static. For these, we brought in a really great prosthetic guy and we custom built the suits for the guys because we wanted to make them as comfortable as possible. The (puppeteers) were bearing anywhere from sixty to eighty pounds and more on their backs, with all the motors and batteries and the weight of the foam rubber suit itself. It was a tremendous accomplishment that they could take those legs, go into that horrible stance and walk around."

Although these babies couldn't travel far, they could

stand and teeter a couple paces. This was enough mobility to allow Emmerich to shoot some scenes with a horde of Baby Godzillas, including a funny moment when a group of hungry infants feast on bags of popcorn in a Madison Square Garden hallway. On Emmerich's cue, the babies munched and chomped as several production assistants tossed handfuls of popcorn into the frame, to simulate a bona fide feeding frenzy.

"We used the guys on stilts for some action but the compromise is if you do action with those guys walking as best as they can and then you match that with CG, CG is going to do better. So, we used this only for one or two shots where there was a group of them and one is walking only two or three steps," Tatopoulos says.

One of the design factors that enabled the Baby Godzillas to stand and saunter was their tail, which featured a springy bungee cord running down the length of it. This allowed the tail to move naturally with the body and counterbalanced the weight of the suit and the weird angle of the stilts.

"When you look at dinosaurs or crocodiles, they don't actually have a tail that does little things all alone, it's just the main drive is in the bottom of the hips of the creature. For example, the crocodile has a big strong muscle that throws the tail, the tail doesn't do anything, it just swings and goes wide. So, if you have the drive on the rear end of the actor and he moves his hips with a tail that actually has a bungee in there, you get the real, natural movement. If you start throwing mechanics (into the suit), it makes it heavier and also it's not coordinated properly in space. So, actually, it makes more sense to have this bungee tail moving around like this. I showed it to Roland and he thought it was the way to go, too. Even on the motion base, we made a dummy tail that bounced around," Tatopoulos explains.

Because Tatopoulos had designed such a sleek creature, there was little space within the suit to bury the mechanisms that would control the movements not controlled by their own legs.

"It was difficult because the motors that we used in the suits had to be very small but really torquey and fast and also respond to the various commands and actions that we wanted to do. That just doesn't exist anywhere in the industry," Himber says. "So, pretty much, all the motor systems and drives had to be retrofitted and custom built in-house. Basically, everything, from the electrical motor system to the cable drive, was based on pieces we begged, borrowed, and stole from other industries and brought them together. We researched and developed them into this beautiful, optimized package that just drove those heads all over the place. They had so much torque in them that we could whip the head around and essentially take the whole guy in the suit with him. The whole thing was self-contained, there were no wires coming off of them, it was all radio controlled."

Himber and crew built this package of controls out of carbon fiber tooling to keep the weight down, especially in the head, where they installed the "gearbox systems and a lot of the electronics." Despite their lizard-like exterior and their human interior, these baby suits were veritable robots.

"We had electronics and cable systems going down the back, an intercom unit in front of them, an air circulation system. Right over the hips, they had a whole series of motors that extended back into the tail section, which was all full of batteries and a few other little goodies," Himber says.

Himber's crew wired the babies first and applied essentially the same technology to "the Mom suit," i.e. the 1/24th-scale animatronic model, which, ironically, was smaller than the babies.

The skin surrounding all these cables, wires and batteries was made of foam rubber, which is not the material they employed on the *Independence Day* aliens. "It's the best material to work with because it has a lot of stretch to it and also has a lot compression. With silicones (the other favored material in the trade), you never get that and they're heavier than hell, too. We'd come off a big, hellish silicone suit on *Independence Day* and we were like, 'Ugh, let's just not do that, it's too much of a pain.' The paint never sticks to it, it's just the worst."

---

■ OPPOSITE PAGE UPPER LEFT: *Details of a mechanical claw being assembled.*

■ OPPOSITE PAGE BOTTOM: *The large-scale tail gets rigged for its moment of glory when it rams the 1/4th-scale model of the bridge of the floating fish factory.*

■ UPPER RIGHT: *The frame for the 1/6th-scale Godzilla's flexible tail.*

■ LOWER RIGHT: *Another view of the tail frame.*

Himber says the biggest challenge he faced on *Godzilla*, quite literally, was the enormous, 1/6th-scale head.

"That big hydraulic character . . . the toughest part was the control system. We tried to make it as smart and safe as possible because it was so big and powerful and potentially crazy and dangerous. We built systems inside that looked for pressure loss and if that happened, they shut the system down, systems that found too much pressure would shut it down too. Systems would find a mismatched signal from the actuator, all these things were basically waiting for problems to happen and we just tread this little tiny path between them, which is the actual working range to get a performance out of it."

The hydraulic baby didn't harbor as many safeguards, as it didn't pose as many potential safety hazards because it was so much smaller than the 1/6th-scale head.

"The hydraulic baby was pretty much direct input/output. If the little guy cut loose and did some crazy stuff, unless you're right next to him, he really could only hurt himself. But, the big one was basically a big, psycho death machine if it let go," Himber says. "There was so much force and momentum behind it." Fortunately, the 1/6th-scale head didn't experience any psychotic episodes during the shoot. Ultimately, these animatronic Godzillas were intermingled with their CG counterparts, although as the film progressed, the filmmakers began to lean more toward the latter. By February 1998, the number of digital effects shots had risen to almost four hundred. "The flexibility that the keyframe animation afforded us, meant that Dean and Roland were constantly rethinking sequences and often-times inventing new ones," says Bull. "Every week handfuls of shots were either shifting from the 'practical' approach to digital or the animation was becoming more and more daring—Godzilla leaping over buildings or the babies slipping and sliding on gumballs."

In order to make the release date and affect all these digital shots, the visual effects strategy altered slightly. Clearly, with the increasing amount of digital shots, Centropolis Effects could not "final" all the shots. All the animating continued to commence at Centropolis Effects, so that Emmerich could approve Godzilla's basic form and movement within scenes, while also cutting the movie, across the hall from Centropolis Effects, with editors, David Siegel, Peter Amundson, and VFX Editor Peter Elliott.

Engel says, "I called CFX our base camp. CFX was definitely our headquarters. The tendency was not to final it here but eighty to ninety percent of the creature and of the Baby Godzillas were done at CFX, the hero shots. It was a different concept than we had in the beginning. We thought we'd have forty percent here, thirty percent there, so that's different. What we'd do is we start with all the basic stuff here in the morning, Karen Goulekas, Andy Jones, Steffen Wild, Fiona Bull and I, we'd have walk throughs, we'd talk to every artist and compositor who is working on the shots. That was a little preparation for the Roland walk-through that happened a little later, when he made all his comments. We'd also have dailies where the guys from CFX, VisionArt, Sony ImageWorks, and Digiscope showed their shots." The biggest positive surprise during the digital postproduction for me personally was, besides working with everybody at our base camp CFX, the working relationship we established with Sony Imagework's Producer Julia Rivas, Supervisor Jerome Chen and their brilliant team.

───────

■ OPPOSITE PAGE TOP TO BOTTOM: *(a) A lot of different passes had to be applied to the wireframe of the CG-creature. This monitor shows the beauty, iridescent, and wet pass. (b) A wireframe of Godzilla. The creature was built out of 800,000 polygons. (c) The flat-shaded creature. This is how Godzilla looks without his skin texture. This version was often used for previsualization. (d) Effects shot: Godzilla steps over the FDR Drive. To create an exact camera-tracking, the data from the matchmove team was applied to this shot. (e) Conny Fauser's finished composite of a shot in which Godzilla scares a lot of people in Wall Street. Roland Emmerich directed the screaming extras in New York and the CG foot and CG debris, enhanced with some stage splash elements were added in digital compositing.*

■ RIGHT: *Adjusting the Godzilla suit model on the performer.*

■ INSET: *Patrick Tatopoulos' "man-in-suit" Godzilla rises out of the destroyed Madison Square Garden like a Phoenix. This element was later digitally composited into a model background of the destroyed "Garden."*

As the first and second units shot the film, the visual effects teams labored to create Godzilla and the explosive results of his visit to New York. In the tradition of *Independence Day*, several Manhattan landmarks met fiery ends, under the supervision of Joe Viskocil. Viskocil's pyrotechnics previously caused the demise of the White House in *Independence Day* and one his first blasts led to the end of the fabled Death Star in *Star Wars*. The difference on *Godzilla*, he notes, is that he and his team, twice the size of the unit he employed on *Independence Day*, imploded rather than exploded the buildings.

"We had mechanical rigs that blasted through a building and then they put in the CG Godzilla later on, but we had to simulate what he does to that building. Most of the time, it was imploding the building. In other words, you're

---

■ TOP SEQUENCE: *The demolition of the "East River Pier" was done via a 1/6th-scale Godzilla head made out of fiberglass. It was running on tracks and pulled by a tow-truck.*

■ INSET: *Emmerich directs the positioning of the fisherman and his rod.*

■ LEFT VERTICAL SEQUENCE: *(a) The fisherman checks his line when he thinks he has hooked a big one. (b) A fisherman casually drinks a beer while waiting for a big strike. (c) The fisherman is terrified by the apparent size of what's on his line.*

■ BELOW: *A storyboard sequence showing the advance plan for the progression of this dramatic episode which was also used for one of the very popular previews months in advance of the movie release.*

■ TOP RIGHT: *View of a model of the top of the Chrysler Building against a screen background.*

■ TOP CENTER RIGHT: *A shot of a pyrotechnic explosion effect showing the destruction of the top of the Chrysler Building.*

■ CENTER: *The actor playing the fisherman in preparation for his big scene.*

■ FAR RIGHT: *Miniature Chrysler Building on set with all rigging around it for shooting.*

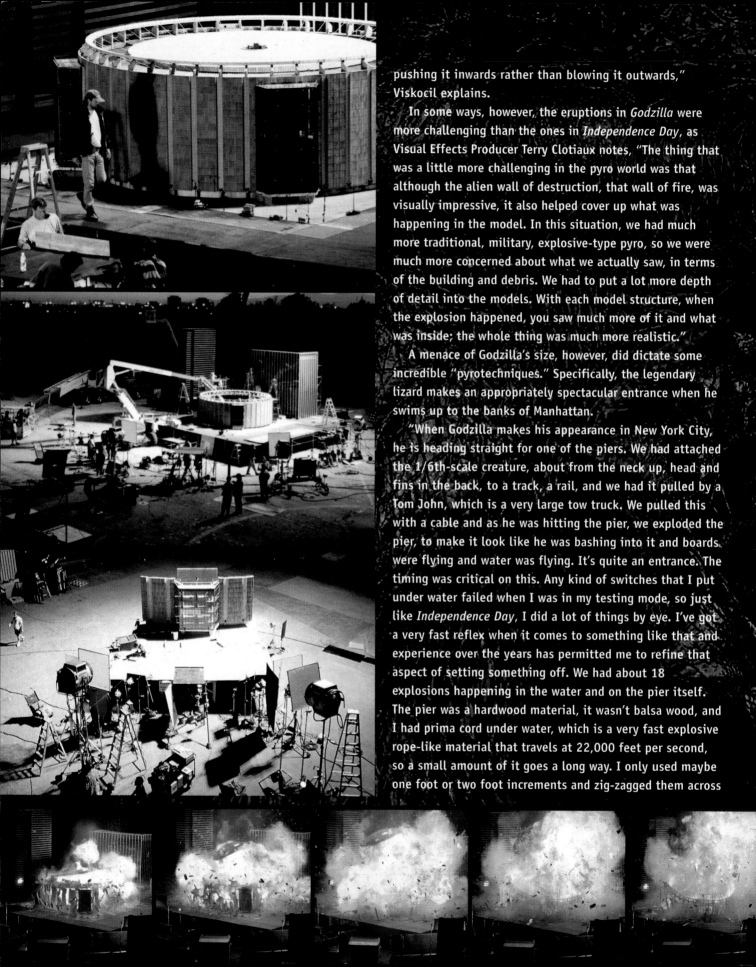

pushing it inwards rather than blowing it outwards," Viskocil explains.

In some ways, however, the eruptions in *Godzilla* were more challenging than the ones in *Independence Day*, as Visual Effects Producer Terry Clotiaux notes, "The thing that was a little more challenging in the pyro world was that although the alien wall of destruction, that wall of fire, was visually impressive, it also helped cover up what was happening in the model. In this situation, we had much more traditional, military, explosive-type pyro, so we were much more concerned about what we actually saw, in terms of the building and debris. We had to put a lot more depth of detail into the models. With each model structure, when the explosion happened, you saw much more of it and what was inside; the whole thing was much more realistic."

A menace of Godzilla's size, however, did dictate some incredible "pyrotechniques." Specifically, the legendary lizard makes an appropriately spectacular entrance when he swims up to the banks of Manhattan.

"When Godzilla makes his appearance in New York City, he is heading straight for one of the piers. We had attached the 1/6th-scale creature, about from the neck up, head and fins in the back, to a track, a rail, and we had it pulled by a Tom John, which is a very large tow truck. We pulled this with a cable and as he was hitting the pier, we exploded the pier, to make it look like he was bashing into it and boards were flying and water was flying. It's quite an entrance. The timing was critical on this. Any kind of switches that I put under water failed when I was in my testing mode, so just like *Independence Day*, I did a lot of things by eye. I've got a very fast reflex when it comes to something like that and experience over the years has permitted me to refine that aspect of setting something off. We had about 18 explosions happening in the water and on the pier itself. The pier was a hardwood material, it wasn't balsa wood, and I had prima cord under water, which is a very fast explosive rope-like material that travels at 22,000 feet per second, so a small amount of it goes a long way. I only used maybe one foot or two foot increments and zig-zagged them across

■ **RIGHT TOP:** *(a) Smoke and flame from a pyrotechnic explosion (b) As the smoke clears the remnant of a miniature building can be seen.*

■ **FAR LEFT FROM TOP TO BOTTOM:** *(a) Volker Engel takes a final look at the "Garden" model before it is blown up. (b) The explosion of the 1/24th-scale Madison Square Garden required a vast space, so the miniature shooting crew set it up on a former helicopter landing pad on the old Hughes Aircraft facility. (c) The 1/10th-scale Madison Square Garden entrance miniature is being prepped on the parking lot outside Hanger 45 where most of the Godzilla miniatures were shot.*

■ **BOTTOM SEQUENCE:** *This series shows the carefully choreographed explosion of the 1/24th-scale Madison Square Garden in all its glory.*

■ **INSET:** *Thousands of tiny chairs had to be built for the interior of the 1/24th-scale Madison Square Garden.*

the pier and, boy, that pier was history," Viskocil says.

Of course, Emmerich and Devlin just couldn't set a movie in Manhattan without blowing up a few landmarks. ("We had so much fun blowing up New York City in *Independence Day* that we decided to come back for more," Devlin quips.) Madison Square Garden was the biggest model to erupt. Its demise didn't proceed exactly according to plan, but the "flaw" in the explosion provided an artistic boon.

"For the explosion of Madison Square Garden we used two different model scales, a huge 1/24th-scale model for the main explosion and a 1/10th-scale one for the detonation of one of the glass towers.

The main detonation was captured with multiple cameras. My DP (Director of Photography) Anna Foerster and her team really had their hands full. It's a nerve-racking task but she had everything completely under control and each angle had perfectly exposed film," Volker Engel recalls.

These different camera angles were later composited with elements of the

113

runnings actors at Digiscope, a company that had already provided lots of spectacular digital composites for Independence Day. "It's so much easier to work with the trusted people you know, like Mary Stewart's team from Digiscope. It's almost like family," says Engel.

The famed Chrysler Building and the Flatiron Building are also crippled in *Godzilla*. Their injuries required lengthy preparation, tests, and considerable choreography.

"Both the Chrysler Building and the Flatiron Building were created by (the model effects company) Hunter-Gratzner and I worked in conjunction with them on the mechanical aspects. In the Chrysler Building, we wanted to rig it so that once the top couple of floors exploded, the tower then shifted and came towards camera, falling. It was tricky and we did it twice. We worked hand in hand with Hunter-Gratzner, working out the mechanics of this platform that has the tip just as it's exploding. Everything happened very fast, but of course on film it happened very

■ **RIGHT:** *Miniature Special Effects Supervisor Joe Viskocil prepares the Chrysler Building spire for the big drop.*

■ **INSET:** *Model maker Mike Woolaway walks along the 35 foot model of a floating fish factory, one of the many highly detailed models built by Cinnabar in Burbank.*

■ **LEFT:** *Visual Effects Supervisor Volker Engel examines the model street set used for the drop of the Chrysler Building spire.*

■ **BOTTOM SEQUENCE LEFT TO RIGHT:**
*(a) Front view of Flatiron Building on set and ready to shoot. (b) Head Pyrotechnician, Joe Viskocil, double checks the electrical charges on the Flatiron Building just before shooting begins. (c) Left, full side of the Flatiron Building on set. (d) Detail shot of lower section of the Flatiron Building, including custom graffiti. (e) Close-up of graffiti area of the Flatiron Building miniature. (f) Hunter Gratzner Industries Supervisor, Matthew Gratzner, installs the last window shade on the Flatiron Building.*

slowly, you see everything," Viskocil says.

"As for the Flatiron Building, that was another one that had a building block on the inside of the whole model, so that it had what we call in the business 'weak knees.' If you pull a pin out of this knee, it will collapse the joint and it will in turn collapse the entire leg of it. So, that had to be worked out. Timing is absolutely critical, especially on something that you're shooting 360 frames per second. So, we did a lot of tests for the timing and the look of the explosions. Once we did those tests, we would take it to Volker and get his approval on it, to see if he wants it bigger or smaller or more debris or less fire or no fire, that sort of thing. Then we'd go do it," Viskocil explains.

The effects department also filmed several model sequences that occurred on water, particularly the three model fishing trawlers, equivalent to the full-scale boat that Godzilla yanks beneath the surface, as well as a "floating fish factory" that attracts the hungry creature. The latter was the first

ABOVE LEFT: *The flooding corridor on the Japanese ship after Godzilla has torn it open.*

ABOVE RIGHT: *A close-up view of Godzilla's claws tearing through the side of the Japanese ship.*

BELOW LEFT TO RIGHT: *(a) In the opening sequence the 35-foot model is attacked by Godzilla and capsizes. (b) In the opening sequence a gigantic hydraulic Godzilla-tail smashes into this detailed quarter-scale miniature of the floating fish-factory's bridge. (c) The fish factory ship model surrounded by workers. (d) Volker Engel examines the fish-factory ship model.*

UPPER RIGHT: *Production Coordinator Patrick Ellis(right) examines the 1/4th-scale fishing boats, built by John Stirber and crew.*

INSET: *Scene inside the Japanese fish-factory ship as Godzilla tears out the side with his claws.*

shot that Volker Engel, Terry Clotiaux, and team attempted. Originally, Emmerich and Devlin had written the barge to be a supertanker that Godzilla attacked, but after some discussion, they altered it to a Japanese fishing operation.

"Two-thirds of the supertanker was already built when the decision was made to change it. Big story point. Godzilla goes for the fish. We were really looking for, why is he attacking this supertanker? He doesn't have any interest in doing that unless it's loaded with fish. Steve Legler, our Visual Effects Art Director, worked closely with our main model-building facility, Cinnabar, to quickly incorporate these changes. Doug Morris and his team of devoted model makers and engineers did an incredible job to turn these changes around in time," Engel says.

The crew filmed this sequence in a tank in Acton, California, which Digital Domain built for *Titanic*. In fact, *Godzilla* and *Titanic* occasionally overlapped in the beginning of the shoot.

"At one point, we actually had both *Titanic* and *Godzilla* in the building shooting at the same time. I wonder how often that's happened, two giant movies together. *Godzilla* and *Titanic*: Could you get much bigger than that? It was pretty amazing," Clotiaux muses.

The first shot in this outdoor tank revolved around the fish factory, sailing through rough seas. Anna Foerster and her fearless cameracrew shot these scenes in a two week marathon under the supervision of Volker Engel and Miniature Effects Supervisor Don Baker.

"It was a small tank and the first thing we had was a stormy night and this huge model and we were in another one of those situations where we've got all these different elements that have to work (simultaneously) to make the illusion work. The light had to hit just right, the water has to look just right, the rain has to look just right, the smoke and fog have to look just right, everything . . . You're shooting forty-five seconds of film and out of that forty-five seconds, when you're shouting 'More smoke, more rain,' you're really looking for those three seconds that make it all magic. That was a location without any support services or systems to speak of at all, so we had to go out and essentially set it up as if it were a location shoot. Lots of problems. When we originally looked at the sequence, we talked about moving the model through water and to do that, we needed a big, big tank. We had talked about using the tank at Paramount and building the whole rig to move it there. We finally came to realize what we were asked to do based on the storyboards, we could actually move the water, keep the boat stationary and move the water. So, that worked for us and Roland was happy," Clotiaux says.

While the team sailed through this sequence with relatively few problems, they were not as lucky with the miniature fishing trawlers, which lensed at

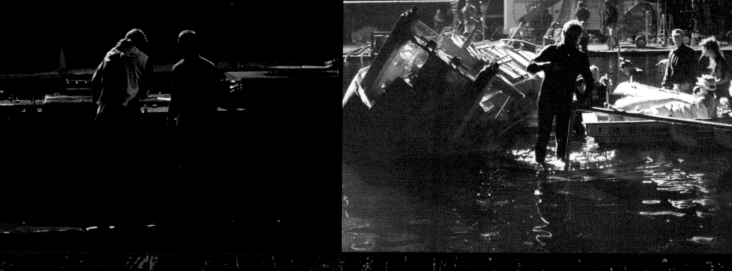

Falls Lake. Just setting up the track and pulley system that, as with the full scale boat, would yank the models underwater was a complicated endeavor.

"The special effects guys were given a very difficult task, in terms of trying to make all this work. We were under a tight schedule. Different rigs had to be placed in the lakebed before we filled it up, so first unit had some of its (pre-rig) stuff there (Falls Lake), we were doing our stuff there, so we had to coordinate between the two shooting teams, how things were being placed at the bottom, the tracking, the pulley systems that had to be worked out and placed in the time period we were allowed before we filled the tank with water. Once we did that, it would be very, very difficult to make changes underwater. We also didn't want time spent draining it and filling it with water. So, it was a challenge to get everything installed at the same time and filling the tank. For the most part, it worked out," Clotiaux says.

The sequence itself was inherently difficult because the model boats

■ TOP LEFT TO RIGHT: *(a) Another view of workers prepping the fish-factory ship model. (b) A side view of the model of the fish-factory ship shown leaning over in the process of capsizing. (c) The model of the fish-factory ship being lowered into the water by crane. (d) A front view of the model of the fish-factory ship shown leaning over in the process of capsizing.*

■ INSET: *Storyboard plan for the trawler resurfacing sequence.*

■ RIGHT: *While making his entrance in New York, Godzilla drops fishing boats that were stuck to his fins. Special effects technician Joe Heffernan hoses down one of the boats that were dropped from a 50-foot crane onto a metal plate. The boat then gets digitally composited into the New York footage.*

had to have two antithetical talents: The ability to float for the establishing shot and the capacity to sink.

Clotiaux continues, "The fishing trawler sequence had an enormous amount of difficulties. We had to build models that had to do a number of gags. They had to move forward like they would under normal operating conditions and pull backwards and then had to pull them under and then they had to pop up. So, we were asking a lot of the models. John Stirber and his team built the models. They looked great and they functioned amazingly well. The problem was that we couldn't get the boats to sink. So we came up with a different system, we ended up utilizing the system that they had set up for first unit. They had to sink the full-sized boats, so we basically took the dolly that they had made and mounted out three boats on it using the same track. I am quick to point out that ours were on a cable system, so they were not hard-mounted, literally the boats were floating and we had to pull them back. The action of pulling them back on the cable system that we had was on a loop powered by this enormous tow truck used for big rigs. You had this pulley system that was hooked up to the Tom John. There was the Tom John on the

# WELL, WE COULD GET ONE DOWN AT THE RIGHT TIME, WE COULD GET TWO DOWN AT THE RIGHT TIME, BUT WE COULD NEVER GET THREE.

land, the boats on the water. He moved forward and they moved, too. The pick point was down deep, so that when he moved this way, it pulled them down. Again, the smoke had to be right, the rain had to be right, everything had to be right and they had to all three go underwater. Well, we could get one down at the right time, we could get two down at the right time, but we could never get three at the right time. We'd been asking these boats to float, float, float up

until that point. Suddenly, we were saying, sink, sink, sink. So, they had a whole air system in them which we had to flood immediately. It was a whole mechanical gag that was trying to work. And we didn't want them to sink too fast. It was a challenge, so putting it back on the track helped. The gag that we ended up using only worked because we had all the previous footage, by putting them on this thing and pulling them down, we could put the two together," Clotiaux says.

Most of the model shots were even more integrated into various components of first unit photography and digital work. A sequence in which Godzilla chases a cab along the Brooklyn Bridge, entangling himself in its girders, is a perfect example of this. Originally, the film team hoped to use a 1/24th-scale man-in-the-suit Godzilla running along a 170-foot model bridge for this sequence. That plan soon changed to a combination of CG and first and second unit live-action, with only a minimal use of the 1/24th-scale suit.

"We thought we would be able to use the 1/24th-scale creature for the showdown on the Brooklyn Bridge. We found out early enough in the process that the 1/24th-scale suit was not performing the way we'd hoped. First of all, the guy couldn't see and second, the feet were constructed so stiff that it looked like a woman on high-heeled shoes running over the bridge. So we decided to build the whole bridge in addition as a model in the computer. We still used the model of the bridge ramp and its two towers for a lot of the model shots. This model and a 1/6th-scale piece for the collapsing bridge was built by Cinnabar under the supervision of model maker Mike Woolaway. For these shots we also utilized radio-controlled replicas of the hero cab. These were driven with a sure hand by Model Shop Supervisor Gene Rizzardi.

"There was a really positive conceptual development while all these changes happened, and, in fact, this enhanced the nature of these shots. CG Animation Supervisor Andy Jones came up with this idea to let Godzilla leap with two gigantic steps on top of the first

bridge tower. He just came up with it and showed it to us the next day. Roland and I were completely stunned. It turned out to be way more spectacular than just having him break through both towers and we could never have done that with the 1/24th-scale suit in the first place," Engel says.

THAT PLAN SOON CHANGED TO A COMBINATION OF CG AND FIRST AND SECOND UNIT LIVE-ACTION.

"We had Andy's animation with the gray flat-shaded Godzilla as a guide, while shooting elements of the model bridge on stage. This process is called previsualization. Every animation was approved by Roland and could be used as reference to whatever had to be shot as a miniature element on stage."

Although Godzilla was now relegated to the CG realm, as was most of the Brooklyn Bridge, his presence had to be taken into account, especially when shooting the bridge's second turret.

"When Godzilla rams through the second bridge tower we used a very unique technique. Based on a still frame from Andy's CG animation, Joe Viskocil's effect crew

■ ABOVE: *The storyboard sequence for the retreat to an abandonned cab as Godzilla pursues the people he believes responsible for destroying his nest and the Baby Godzilla hatchlings.*

■ UPPER LEFT: *Overhead view of Godzilla's foot destroying cars on a New York street.*

■ LOWER LEFT: *The 1/24th-scale Brooklyn Bridge is being set up in Hangar 15. Not a single shot in the movie was shot on the real bridge.*

■ RIGHT: *Modelmaker Tony Ciccarelli prepares a freeway sign on the 1/24th-scale Brooklyn Bridge.*

■ LEFT: *A shot from the cab chase sequence.*

■ RIGHT: *Baby Godzilla eggs for the miniature "Madison Square Garden" interior had to be created in two sizes: For foreground and background.*

■ BELOW: *A green-screen Godzilla shape crashes through the second Brooklyn Bridge tower. In the movie the green shape will later be replaced by a computer-generated Godzilla.*

constructed a rigid metal Godzilla which was running on tracks and could slice through the bridge tower like a knife through butter. For this stunt, model maker Mike Woolaway incorporated a lot of breakaway sections into the six-foot-tall tower.

The 'Mecha-Godzilla' was painted with bright green color. This color matched exactly the one from the huge green screen that was rigged as a background. In digital compositing, the color green would be subtracted so that only the tower and all falling debris pieces would be visible. The background would be replaced with a night sky and the green metal creature with

WE CONSTRUCTED A GREEN GODZILLA MARKER, WHICH HAD

THE BASIC GODZILLA SHAPE. IT LOOKED REALLY BIZARRE.

the detailed CG Godzilla. There would still be a ton of hand-rotscoping, but all the basics were there. This could be easily the most spectacular shot in the movie. A perfect match of traditional model work, highspeed photography and high-end computer animation. The best of all worlds."

All this was meshed with the first unit photography, which took place in downtown Los Angeles, along the Seventh Street Bridge, as well as a second unit sequence, filmed near the Torrance Airport in Los Angeles. There, a section of the Brooklyn Bridge emerged from a corn field, over which a cab would speed from Godzilla's grasp.

"We replicated four hundred feet of the Brooklyn Bridge. It is so cool. That was based on photographs and we took that over and had it scaled by the draftsmen. We figured out a component system that would expedite building it because it was quite complex, with two million rivets and cross braces and all that. We tried to simplify that with various molds, but it was 400 feet long, 30 feet wide, and 15 feet tall. We couldn't do that in miniature because we had to use a real car and it had to support it," says Construction Coordinator P. Gary Krakoff.

A shift of the camera and an ample layer of smoke obscured the pastoral setting surrounding this

---

■ LEFT TOP: *Visual Effects Director of Photography Anna Foerster operates a camera when the 1/6th-scale Godzilla bites a piece out of the Brooklyn Bridge onramp. A detailed replica of the New York taxicab is carefully positioned between the jaws.*

■ LEFT CENTER: *A real cab gets smashed by a gigantic metal plate. This element was used for the end-sequence of the movie.*

■ LEFT BOTTOM: *Crushed cab and the steel plate used to do the actual smashing.*

■ RIGHT CLOCKWISE FROM TOP: *(a) Godzilla's foot about to crush a crowd of people. (b) Godzilla appears and the crowds flee in panic. (c) An effects shot in preparation stage shows falling debris which is later composited into the final shot. (d) Godzilla comes around a corner as*

■ LEFT TOP: *For G*
*entrance into Wall*
*model crew pushed*
*stone debris from t*
*destroyed Flatiron*
*through some stack*
*wooden panels. Thi*
*was later composite*
*of a live-action sho*
*Wall Street.*

■ LEFT CENTER: *A*
*the crumpled cab.*

■ LEFT BOTTOM: *N*
*foreground standing*
*of the crumpled cab*

■ RIGHT TOP: *A sh*
*Animal, Nick, and A*
*the aftermath of Go*
*final destruction.*

■ RIGHT BOTTOM:
*Audrey watch in sho*
*Godzilla's rampage*
*an end.*

■ INSET: *Nick and*
*kiss as their differe*
*resolved by the end*
*Godzilla.*

Brooklyn Bridge West and at one point,
seven cameras rolled to catch the action.
Co-producer Peter Winther helmed this
unit and points out that, despite the
advances in the computer world, the
brief but incisive use of "reality" helps
authenticate the final sequence.

"If you hold too long on a model shot
or a computer image, audiences realize
that's what they are seeing. It sells the
shot more if you intercut it with live-
action, which is why we built the
bridge and used a real car for
certain shots. It's all
sleight of hand, really,"
Winther notes.

This portion of
the Brooklyn
Bridge sequence,
with its movie
trucks, cameras,
lights, cables,
generators,
smoke machines,
rain rigs and
fans, as well as
the piece of bridge
itself, all juxtaposed
against a patch of grass
and wild flowers, exemplified
the uneasy balance between man's
technology and nature. This precarious
equilibrium tilts in favor of nature when
Godzilla appears, as Emmerich observes.

"I see it as a fight between nature and
technology," Emmerich adds. "When you
try to capture a creature or hunt it down,
if it is small, then it is easy. But, this is a
big animal; every footstep is 140 feet and
he runs about 300 mph. It's not so easy
to catch something that runs that fast in
New York City. You have to figure out
what kind of equipment and weaponry
you need to catch the thing without
blowing up the whole city. That's the kind
of problem New York has, but every
animal is smart and so is Godzilla. It
learns from its mistakes."

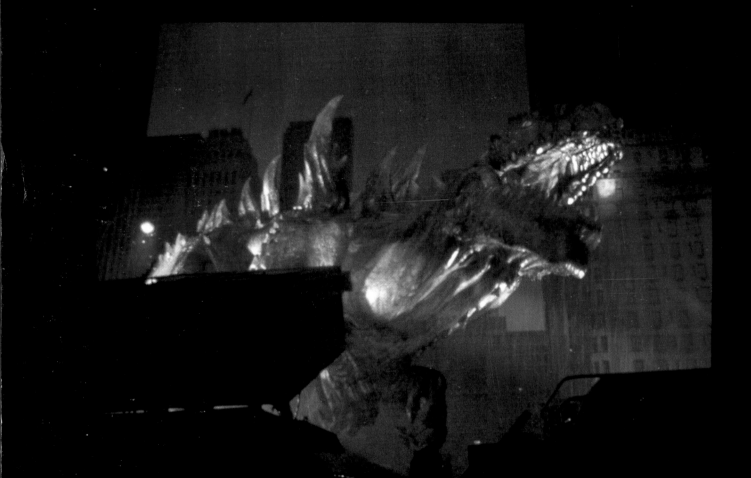